WAR AND FAITH IN SUDAN

WAR AND FAITH IN SUDAN

Gabriel Meyer

With photographs by

James Nicholls

WILLIAM B. EERDMANS PUBLISHING COMPANY
GRAND RAPIDS, MICHIGAN / CAMBRIDGE, U.K.

Wm. B. Eerdmans Publishing Co.
255 Jefferson Ave. S.E., Grand Rapids, Michigan 49503 /
P.O. Box 163, Cambridge CB3 9PU U.K.
www.eerdmans.com

Printed in the United States of America

10 09 08 07 06 05   7 6 5 4 3 2 1

Library of Congress Cataloging-in-Publication Data

Meyer, Gabriel, 1947-
War and faith in Sudan / Gabriel Meyer;
with photographs by James Nicholls
p.   cm.
Includes bibliographical references and index.
ISBN 0-8028-2933-3 (cloth: alk. paper)
1. Nuba (African people) — Social conditions.
2. Nuba Mountains Region (Sudan) — Social conditions.
I. Nicholls, James.   II. Title.

DT155.2.N82M49   2005
962.8 — dc22

2005050712

Excerpt from AHEAD OF ALL PARTING by Rainer Maria Rilke,
translated by Stephen Mitchell, copyright © 1995 by Stephen Mitchell.
Used by permission of Modern Library, a division of Random House, Inc.

To the memory of the children of Kauda

and all the victims

of Sudan's second civil war (1983-2005)

Contents

Foreword

Gabriel Meyer has written a truly remarkable book, a story told by a man who started as a reporter grudgingly drawn into covering a war — the latest of the human brutalities he had covered in several regions of the world — from which he would have preferred to disengage. Instead, under the spell of the persuasive Bishop Macram Max Gassis, Meyer not only became intimately involved with the tragedies of that war, but developed such a strong identification with the people and their cause that toward the end of the saga and the book, one of the local leaders asked him, "Don't you know that you are part of us?"

Interposed with graphic and moving photographs by James Nicholls, the story Meyer has to tell in *War and Faith in Sudan* is painfully gripping, not only in what it says, but also in how it is told, narrated in factually descriptive yet poetic language that engulfs the reader with its own intrinsic power. Well researched, the story has an eloquent and elegant flow that welds together mythology about the origins of the Nuba people, their history, their culture, and their place in the turbulent, indeed terroristic context of modern Sudan and its genocidal wars of identities. It is a story that profoundly blends journalism with scholarship, literature, and a sharp sense of the political dynamics that link the local with the global in a crisis that, though initially ignored by the outside world, has eventually drawn international attention.

Although the focus of the book is on the Nuba, Meyer covers the whole Sudan, a theater of multilayered conflicts that have at their roots an acute crisis of national identity. The first layer, pitting the Arab-

Muslim North against the African Christian and so-called "animist" South, erupted in 1955, was halted in 1972 by a precarious peace agreement that granted the South limited regional autonomy, and resumed in 1983 when the government unilaterally abrogated that agreement. While the first war was separatist, the declared objective of the second, championed by the Sudan People's Liberation Movement and Army (SPLM/A), was and continues to be the restructuring of the country to be free from discrimination on the basis of race, ethnicity, religion or culture.

This recasting of the issues eventually began to gain support in the North, especially in the non-Arab regions. The Nuba of Southern Kordofan and the Ingassana or Funj of Southern Blue Nile were the first to join the SPLM/A in the struggle. In 1991, a group of Darfurians, with the support of the SPLM/A, staged a rebellion that proved naively premature and was ruthlessly suppressed by the Sudan government armed forces. Twelve years later, two non-Arab groups in Darfur, the Justice and Equality Movement (JEM) and the Sudan Liberation Movement and Army (SLM/A), staged a second, more devastating and sustained rebellion. While the situation of the Beja in the East has not exploded to the same degree as that of the Nuba Mountains, Southern Blue Nile, and Darfur, it remains precarious and could, if not well managed, erupt into another violent front. Even the Nubians in the far north, the closest to the Arab world, have organized movements opposed to the old status quo, are reviving their pride in their Nubian identity, and are sharing the vision of a restructured Sudan propounded by the SPLM/A.

The paradox is that the crisis in Darfur erupted while the war between the government and the SPLM/A (which includes the Nuba and the Ingessana or Funj) was on its way to a constructive resolution through a peace process brokered by the Inter-Governmental Authority for Development (IGAD), with the support of the United States in a four-way partnership with Italy, Norway, and the United Kingdom. The Comprehensive Peace Agreement (CPA), which was signed in the Kenyan capital, Nairobi, on January 9, 2005, stipulates that the people of the South will have the right to decide by referendum whether to secede or remain united with the North, while the people of the Nuba Mountains and Southern Blue Nile will be granted regional autonomy and their views on the agreement will be ascertained through "popular consultation," implying a form of "internal self-determination with the framework of national unity."

War and Faith in Sudan is primarily a documentation of the war, mostly in the Nuba Mountains, but it is also about an extraordinary humanitarian, Bishop Macram Max Gassis. In Sudan's wars of identities, which dichotomize the people into a racial and cultural dualism between Arabs and Africans, Gassis would be considered a member of the dominant Arab group that is victimizing the Africans. Yet he has chosen to identify with the underdogs, the Africans, to help protect and assist them and, on their behalf, to reach out and touch the conscience of the global community.

His example has inspired dedicated individuals around the world, particularly in the United States, to stand in unwavering solidarity and partnership with him in support of his mission for the people of his diocese. This is, indeed, a story of persons taking risks on behalf of people they do not know, recognizing their dispossession and persecution, and accepting them as fellow human beings who deserve to be assisted and protected as children of God and members of the human family.

The story of the Nuba is the story of the Sudan in microcosm, a country torn apart by an acute crisis of national identity. At the heart of this crisis is the construction of a mythical notion of a monolithic racial, cultural, and religious identity that has distorted the complex pluralist realities of the country into a simplistic dualism, categorizing the country into Africans and Arabs — a fictional notion of Arabism that welds Arab race and culture and the religion of Islam into a composite whole. The result is that a people who, at best, are an Afro-Arab admixture, are conditioned to claim the purity of Arab ancestral origin, and even to place non-Arab Muslims into that constructed mold.

The identities currently in conflict arose through an historical evolution in which slavery was a defining factor in classifying groups along racial, religious, and cultural lines: one either belonged to a superior class of masters or to an inferior one of slaves. The broader context of Arabization and Islamization provided the framework for the belief in the dignity of being a Muslim and an Arab, as opposed to a black African, a heathen, and a potential, if not actual, slave. This evolution eventually crystallized into the emergence of the Arab-Muslim North and the indigenous African South.

The North, two-thirds of the country's land and population, is inhabited by members of various ethnic groups, the dominant among whom intermarried with incoming Arab male migrants and traders, and, over centuries, produced a mixed African-Arab racial group that resembles the African peoples below the Sahara. Indeed, the Arabic phrase *Bilad al-Sudan,* from which the country derives its name, means "land of the blacks" and refers to all of those sub-Saharan territories. Arab immigration and settlement in the South, in contrast to the North, were discouraged by natural environmental barriers, the difficulties of living conditions, including the harshness of the tropical climate for people accustomed to the desert, and the resistance of the Nilotic warrior tribes. Those Arabs who ventured southward were primarily slave raiders, who were not interested in Arabizing and Islamizing the southerners, as that would have removed their prey from *dar al-harb* (land of war) and placed them in *dar al-Islam* (land of Islam and peace), thereby liberating them from slavery. The present northern Sudanese identity is therefore the culmination of a process in which the Arab-Muslim identity has been promoted, in the words of one source, as "the best nation God has created."

The northern Sudanese "Arabs," being neither white nor typically black, have given their brown color of skin the description "green," a color of contextualized pride, while they consider "black" and its more polite version, "blue," to be the colors of slaves. Ironically, it has been argued that exaggerated pride in Arabism stems from an underlying inferiority complex associated with the African connection. After all, most Sudanese "Arabs" have some slave blood in them, whereas black Africans who successfully resisted or escaped slavery are paradoxically viewed by those bearing the marks of slave background as the slaves. In the words of Mansour Khalid, a prominent Sudanese scholar, diplomat, and statesman, "The reason [for northern pride in Arabism] stems from an inferiority complex, really. The northern Sudanese is torn internally in his Arab-African personality. As a result of his Arabic Islamic cultural development, he views himself in a higher status from other Sudanese not exposed to this process. Arabism gives him his sense of pride and distinction and that is why he exaggerates when he professes it. He becomes more royal than the King, so to speak." By the same token, the northern Sudanese elite have not been able to understand why southerners have resisted Arabization and Islamization, which they see as a means of elevating southerners from an inferior, denigrated status to a level of higher culture, civilization, and dignity.

Even the purely non-Arab groups in the North, such as the Nuba and the Fur, were made or taught to believe that they were of Arab stock, should identify as Arabs, and ought to take pride in that racial and cultural heritage as part of a process of self-enhancement. The late Yusuf Kuwa Mekki, the SPLM Governor of Southern Kordofan — Nuba territory — used to tell the story, recounted in this book, about how schoolchildren were taught to glory in their Arab ancestry. Kuwa believed himself to be Arab until secondary school. "That is what we were taught," he said. "As I understood what was happening and became politically conscious, I recognized that I was Nuba, not Arab."

On the other hand, as the brutality against the Nuba and the non-Arab Darfurians suggests, the conflict may well be more ferocious when it divides people who had otherwise been assumed to be closely connected with the dominant Arab identity. The Darfurians and most Nuba and Ingassana are Muslims and, in the conventional Sudanese way of viewing identity, Islam, Arab culture, and Arab ethnicity or race, are closely connected. Indeed, before the SPLM/A postulated the vision of the New Sudan, the government army that was fighting in the South was predominantly composed of soldiers from the Nuba Mountains and Darfur, fighting to defend — and sometimes impose — the Arab-Muslim hegemony in the country. The resumption of the war with redefined objectives that are embracing of all the marginalized groups, for the most part non-Arabs, began to change the dynamics of identification in a fundamental way.

It is in this context that the Nuba and the Darfurians, who had been viewed as part of the Arab-Islamic North and a source of their best fighting men in defense and imposition of that identity, could be viewed by the self-styled Arabs as having betrayed the cause and come to pose an even greater threat to the establishment than the South.

Such ambiguities of identity have potential to be either acutely divisive or bridging. With the framework of the New Sudan postulated by the SPLM/A, the realignment and bridging processes have begun to develop. Many "Arabs" are increasingly acknowledging their African links. However, with these strategic shifts, the "losing" side, in this case the assumed Arab identity, naturally feels betrayed and threatened. This may well be the precarious position of the Nuba and other non-Arab northern Sudanese groups, who represent both bridging grounds and points of confrontation between African and Arab cultural identity. Hence the brutality with which the government has pursued its counterinsurgency measures against them.

On the same theme of contradictions and ironies, most observers of the Sudanese scene and the character of the people have often commented on the paradox of a people who are so gentle, kind, generous, and hospitable to foreigners in their land, and yet dreadfully ferocious, brutal, and inhumane in their treatment of their own compatriots. The renowned scholar of Sudanese history, Robert O. Collins, has emphasized the positive aspect:

> It really does not matter which particular government is in power — parliamentarian, military, or Islamist — it is the daily encounters with the warmth, charm, and friendliness of the Sudanese of every ethnicity I have known that makes them unique among the people of the world. I have asked myself many times what makes them so affectionate, helpful, and hospitable, and I have no answer. I do know that I cannot recall any westerner who has not established a deep affection for the Sudanese while at the same time cursing the "bloody country." I have never found anyone who can produce a satisfactory answer for his love of the Sudanese that appears an irrational emotion so common among expatriates that it is jokingly regarded as an incurable disease called "Sudanitis. . . ."

The critical question is why a people who are so highly acclaimed for their humanistic virtues can be so inhumane in their treatment of each other internally. The answer must go back to the crisis of national identity that has been the feature of the racial conflicts in the country. Conflicts of identity tend to be inherently zero-sum. The survival with dignity of one identity threatens to denigrate, diminish, and perhaps eliminate the other. Of course, it is not the mere fact of these differences that generates conflicts, but their implications for participation in the shaping and sharing of power, wealth, social services, development opportunities, and the overall enjoyment of the rights and dignity of citizenship. Diversity, compounded by extreme disparity, privileges certain groups and marginalizes other groups into a status of virtual statelessness. This is the core of the genocidal conflicts that have ravaged the country for half a century, initially in the South, and since the mid-1980s in the Nuba Mountains and Southern Blue Nile, and more recently in the western region of Darfur.

The treatment of the people from the South, the Nuba, and Darfur reveals a remarkably common thread of inhumane torture, unabashedly based on racial denigration and dehumanization. An example will prove the point. Chief Stephen Thongkol Anyijong of the Atwot tribe was arrested because he was suspected for sympathy with the southern rebels as a result of information furnished by an Arab trader with whom he had a hostile encounter:

> I stayed jailed for about two years. I just lay there. I did not bathe. I had no clothes to change. And I lay on the floor. It was . . . a house full of insects, dead insects, and all kinds of dead things. . . . My cell was the place into which people were brought when they died. When bodies rotted, they were taken to be thrown wherever they were thrown. Another man would be killed the following day and would be brought into my cell. . . . They beat me and beat me. Hot red pepper was put into my eyes. I said, "Why don't you shoot me, kill me and get it over with? Why do you subject me to this slow death?" They said, "You have to talk." I said, "What do you want me to say?" They said, "You have to say that this idea of the South wanting to be a separate country is something you do not believe in and that you will never support it. . . . You have to swear to that. . . . You will not be left alone until you swear by both the Bible and the [Sacred] Spear." I said, "How can I swear when the whole South is angry? When so many Southerners are in jail? How can I swear that the South will not be separate when this is what everybody wants? This cannot be."

Nor was the fate of Chief Thongkol exceptional; if anything, it was the norm in the South. Mansour Khalid, the prominent northern Sudanese statesman quoted earlier, observed, "The anger of the military was directed against the [insurgents] and the civilian population alike, in both rural and urban centers; villages were burnt down and centers for tortures were established."

In the area of the Ngok Dinka of Abyei, in what was then western Kordofan state, part of Bishop Gassis' diocese, which had historically been something of a North-South bridge, hostilities began to erupt by the mid-1960s. As far as the Arabs were concerned, the conflict was with the ethnic southerners, the Ngok Dinka included The atrocities against the Ngok Dinka of Abyei became widespread as the Arab militias, supported by government security forces, terrorized the population, burning villages, killing, looting, and displacing masses. As is often the case among the Dinka, the experience was recorded in songs of lamentation, complaining to God for having abandoned them:

> How does the spoiling of the world come about?
> Our land is closed in a prison cell.
> The Arabs have spoiled our land,
> Spoiled our land with bearded guns,
> Guns which thunder and then even sound beautiful
> Like the ancient drums with which buffaloes were charmed
> Until their horns were caught.
> Is the black color of skin such a terrible thing
> That the Government should draw its guns?
> The police pacing up and down,
> Gunners causing dust to rise,
> Cowards surrendering to the arm?
> A country we took back from foreigners,
> A country for which we fought together,
> And the English left our country
> Only to be attacked with bren-guns.
> What a treatment!
> O what a treatment . . .
> Our case is in Court with [the spirits] above.

The Court is convened between the clouds . . .
[Our ancestral spirits] have a cause.
They convened the Court
And called upon God:
"God, why are you doing this [to us]?
Don't you see what has become of the black skin?"

The conflict continued to escalate, leading to abduction of women and children into slavery, which the government denies or seeks to mitigate by labeling it "abductions," and the virtual depopulation of the area.

From the mid-1980s, as the war began to spread to the North, beginning with the Nuba, what had been viewed as a conflict confined to the South began to afflict the non-Arab North with identical degradation and dehumanization. The experience of the Nuba became identical to that of those farther South. Meyer's story of Agostino el-Nur Ibrahim, a Nuba who was arrested detained and tortured for being a Christian, sounds very much like that of Chief Thongkol and numerous other southerners:

> I was arrested there on April 14, 1985 and taken to Heiban. I spent one week there under torture. They tied me up with ropes and chains and beat me, there were lashings. Quit being a Christian, they said, and close your church. After that, I was transferred to Kadugli. The conditions there were worse. Christianity is not the religion for Sudan, they said, it's a religion for foreigners. What have you got to do with this religion of infidels? Others said, Repent, if you die, you'll leave your children fatherless. One officer offered me money and a house in Khartoum if I would change my religion.

And as the tragedy spread to Darfur, the same themes of torture continued to be repeated. Abdel Wahid Mohamed Ahmed Nour, who was to become the leader of the Sudan Liberation Movement and Army (SLM/SLA), issued an appeal from prison on August 9, 2002, which the British journalist Julie Flint, one of the individuals who were most instrumental in drawing international attention to Darfur, published in the Parliamentary Brief of July 2004:

I am making this appeal from my cell in Zalingei Security Forces detention centre. The cell space is 16 square meters and is overcrowded: there are 12 of us in this small room without ventilation or windows. . . . Food is very scarce. . . . I have only one lung and I am diabetic. When I was arrested I was suffering from malaria. The security forces refused to allow me to see a doctor.

I would also like to highlight the suffering of my people, the Fur. . . . The security forces act with virtual immunity, terrorizing the Fur people, raiding randomly and arresting people including the elderly and children, detaining them without charge or trail. Many have been subjected to torture. Many Fur men have fled to the mountains to find a safe haven and have left their lands. The Arab tribes attack their lands, looting their properties and stealing their livestock. Many Fur villages have been completely deserted. . . . I call upon the international community and human rights organizations to intervene to free us and protect the people of Darfur from the aggression of the Government.

Meyer has correctly observed that "The Western media seems intent on viewing Darfur as an isolated atrocity; but, in fact, it's part of a much larger, and more complicated evil," which began in the South, spread northward to the Nuba Mountains and Southern Blue Nile, and then to Darfur. Developments in the Beja area and even in Nubia indicate that the cancer continues to spread throughout Sudan's body-politic. There is now abundant evidence to support the argument that the recasting of the objectives of the liberation struggle by the SPLM/A from secession to an equitable restructuring of the country to be free from discrimination on the ground of race, ethnicity, religion, culture, or gender has caught the imagination of the nation and is gaining significant support throughout the North, not only among the non-Arab groups that have been almost equally marginalized and discriminated against, but also among men and women of goodwill in the Arab North, who are concerned with the destiny of the nation.

Ironically, the Nuba Mountains was to play a catalytic role in the peace process that culminated in the Comprehensive Peace Agreement (CPA), signed by the Government of Sudan and the SPLM/A on

January 9, 2005. Amidst the humanitarian crisis in the Nuba Mountains, the United States became actively involved in the peace process. President Bush appointed former Senator John Danforth as his Special Envoy on the Sudan to assess the extent to which the parties wanted peace and what the United States might do to assist the peace process. Danforth used a low-key approach, building on the humanitarian cease-fire, with a focus on the situation in the Nuba Mountains. He pressed the parties to conclude a cease-fire agreement. Final talks in the Swiss town of Burgenstock, mediated by Ambassador Josef Bucher of Switzerland, who had a long-standing involvement in the search for peace in the Sudan, resulted in the signing of the Nuba Mountains Cease-fire Agreement on January 19, 2002. Having achieved a humanitarian cease-fire in the Nuba Mountains, which held remarkably well, supported by a Joint Monitoring Mission and a Joint Military Mission, USAID became intensely engaged in providing humanitarian assistance to the Nuba. This remarkable success on the humanitarian front, with an internationally monitored cease-fire, incrementally expanded to other war-affected areas and eventually connected with the IGAD-sponsored peace process, in which Senator Danforth continued to play an increasingly pivotal role. While many personalities contributed to the ultimate success of the process, the role of the United States and Senator Danforth in particular is acknowledged as having been crucial to the outcome. The United States is likely to remain pivotal to the successful implementation of the Peace Agreement.

While the Comprehensive Peace agreement gives the people of the South the right to decide by a referendum, after a six-year interim period, whether to remain within a united Sudan or to secede and become an independent state, it is hoped that efforts will be exerted during the interim period by both the government of Sudan and the international community to make unity attractive. The agreement also makes special arrangements for the Abyei, Nuba Mountains, and Southern Blue Nile areas, which have been allied with the South in the SPLM/A and which have been equally devastated by the war. As Dr. John Garang de Mabior, leader of the SPLM/A, put it, "The Comprehensive Peace Agreement is a unique Sudanese achievement that I believe shall forever change Sudan as well as have a fundamental and positive impact on our region and Africa."

While most southerners, given a choice today, would overwhelmingly vote for secession, internal and international dynamics may well influence the outcome after the six-year interim period. Internally, the fact that non-Arab regions in the North are rising up with grievances of marginalization, racial discrimination, and economic neglect not dissimilar to what the South has suffered and fought against, may well persuade southerners that they are not alone and that with their allies in the North, they could play a crucial role in restructuring the national identity framework to be equitable and significantly ensure their representation and participation in the shaping and sharing of national power, wealth, services, and development opportunities. Rather than break away as a small, land-locked country, southerners, in partnership with their marginalized non-Arab compatriots, may see value in being partners in Africa's largest and potentially most powerful nation.

War and Faith in Sudan is a book that, in the very nature of the situation it describes, makes for painful, but engaging, reading. What the Sudanese, a people otherwise widely known for their good, friendly, and generous nature, have done to one another sounds, for the most part, unbelievably inhuman. And yet, there is a silver lining to this tragedy. The conflicts that have erupted in non-Arab regions of the North indicate that what is unfolding on the ground reflects a nation in painful search of itself, exploding the divisive old myths of identity and exploring new bases for developing an equitably, inclusive national framework of peace and unity, based on justice and dignity for all. This mounting pressure for equality is challenging the Arab-dominated center to respond creatively and constructively, or risk eventual violent overthrow by the convergence of rebellious regional forces that represent the majority of the country. Ironically, the people of the Nuba Mountains and Darfur, whom the Arab center has used in the past in its failed attempt to Arabize and Islamize the South, may well prove to be the glue that will keep the nation together, but on a completely redefined basis. The transformation taking place on the ground and in which the role of the Nuba has been pivotal, indicates that the vision of the New United Sudan is no longer utopian but an achievable objective. Indeed, it is already unfolding in a dramatic way on the ground.

FRANCIS M. DENG

Francis Deng served as the Representative of the United Nations Secretary General on Internally Displaced Persons from 1992 to 2004; he currently directs the Center for Displacement Studies at John Hopkins University and is a distinguished visiting scholar at the John Kluger Center of the Library of Congress. Prof. Deng is a former Sudanese minister of state for foreign affairs and former Sudanese ambassador to Canada, the United States. and Scandinavia. Among other works, he is the author of the landmark 1995 study War of Visions: Conflict of Identities in the Sudan *(Brookings Institution).*

A Note on the Photographs

Why, in these days of terror and confusion and disillusionment, am I going to try to convince you to spend some time studying photographs of the Nuba people of Sudan? How will it improve your life to immerse yourself in photos of famine and poverty and the ravages of civil war? Surely, there must be one hundred things you'd rather do or need to do than look at the faces of children who have lost their limbs to air attacks by their own government: a walk would be nice. Return some phone calls. You could be or should be cleaning out the garage, or paying the bills; you could be napping, and should be finalizing next summer's vacation plans. You can even be volunteering at the local soup kitchen, taking care of your own poor. But instead, I'm asking you to sit down with Jim Nicholls's photographs, with these people of Sudan, and I'm promising you that good things will spring from this.

Nicholls rather accidentally ended up in the Nuba Mountains with a friend, Gabriel Meyer, and his camera, and what the theologian Howard Thurman calls "quiet eyes." He found the people to be rich in dignity and tradition and goodness. And without meaning to, he fell in love. He fell in love with some of the people you are going to see on these pages: people living lives that their ancestors lived, tending to their livestock and crops, worshiping God, tending to each other, and fighting back, fighting for their freedom in ragtag Salvation Army clothes. He took their pictures to bear witness.

And he took their pictures because they are so beautiful and their story is so heartbreaking and exhilarating. He took their pictures because when you can't fix a tragedy, maybe you can at least honor it. He took them because he believed that these people should not be wiped off the face of the earth without the rest of us knowing it, and acknowledging it. Those of us thousands of miles away in the safety of our homes know on some deeply felt human level that these atrocities are going on, even when we cannot bear to really take it in — but it doesn't help our spirits or our children's to pretend it doesn't exist. The point of this book is not to bog down right now in how deeply implicated we are in their suffering, in self-flagellation because our comforts are based on the misery of others. The point of this book is that the opportunity to alleviate some of that suffering begins with LOOKING. It begins with a willingness to notice, and then noticing for as long as you can bear; to look until you feel joy at the sweetness of these faces, the despair, the nurturing, the posturing of the teenagers, the determination of the parents and the raggedy soldiers to protect the villages. To look until you can see that these people are spiritually our cousins, living just down the road in 130-degree heat; to look until you can understand how each of their fates really matters. It can bring something dead in us back to life, to spend some time with these people.

Look at the soldiers, for instance, the small rebel army that has frequently managed to fight off the soldiers and planes from Khartoum. They appear so pathetic at first, turned out in their crazy secondhand clothes. But look how straight they stand, the strength of their determination, their centeredness. In lieu of weapons and machines, this is what they have to fight with. It's a lot. They stand as tall as aspen, a forest of thin fathers and brothers who are saying, This is what needs to be done, and we will do it.

Look at the face of the little girl with the amulet and the beads and leather necklace during church. She popped up out of nowhere during an Easter Service where Jim was worshiping. Notice the joy, the connection to the spirit as it comes through her. But notice too the look of dubious concern, the slightly rumpled forehead, down cast eyes — shuttered eyes — that look like they could spill over. And the fingers held up to receive the spirit, in a land where so many children don't have fingers or arms. Her small fingers are simultaneously grasping and letting go, palms wide but fingers poised around something invisible, the way you might hold a butterfly.

Over and over in these exquisite photographs, you'll see joy and depression together. Children who have been gravely injured, in their bodies and beings, and you'll see children being nursed and claimed. You'll see a way of life, the housing and churches and fields, you'll see musicians and dancing: such hungry, beleaguered people, with children often starving and the planes overhead, and yet they keep dancing.

So why look through another book of Africans barely surviving? Well, why read another poem? Why take another strenuous hike? Why visit a friend, who despite your tender presence, is going to die anyway? Because that's why we're here, to find out about life, to experience our humanity more deeply. We're here to pay attention, bear witness, and find our way to an authentic relationship with spirit. We're here to grieve and cheer for one another and crack open our hearts, even though that often hurts terribly — Leonard Cohen said that there are cracks in everything, and that that's how the light gets in. So Jim Nicholls gives us these photographs from a remote part of Africa, so we can see her cracks and her light and her shadows — and see our own.

ANNE LAMOTT

Acknowledgments

This book began as a journey. As such, it is proper, first of all, to thank my guides. Chief among these was the person under whose auspices I visited the Nuba: His Excellency Macram Max Gassis, bishop of El Obeid Diocese, Sudan. However much I owe to the good bishop — and that is a great deal — he cannot be held responsible for my impressions or the analytical asides I have ventured to make. Mine is in no way an "official" or authorized account of the work of this legendary churchman.

His staff in Nairobi, past and present, especially Ferdinand von Habsburg, Roberto Bronzino, along with the Rev. Pasquale Boffelli, Michael Nyamori, Francis Mutia and Sharon de Souza, and the directors of the Bishop Gassis Sudan Relief Fund in the U.S., especially Neil Corkery and Dr. David Coffey, were unfailingly generous with their time and resources. Also, I would be remiss if I did not thank Bishop Gassis's friend and colleague Eugenia Canaan and her son Selim for their support and hospitality.

William Saunders, a civil rights attorney in Washington, D.C., led, along with many others, a major effort in the late 1990s to publicize the plight of the Nuba and other marginalized peoples of Sudan. I will always be grateful for his leadership in this effort.

I have also had the counsel of other living "Virgils," including Daniel Kodi Angelo, a Nuba political leader now living in Nairobi, and with whom I traveled to the Nuba Mountains in 1999, Neroun Phillip of the Nuba Relief, Rehabilitation, and Development Organization, and the great Sudanese scholar Francis M. Deng, whose book *War of Visions* was my first introduction to modern Sudanese political history, all of whom have honored me with their friendship. I have also had the deep good fortune to know Sudan's former Minister of Culture and Information, Bona Malwal, and his family, particularly his son Akuei. Professor Jok Madut Jok of Loyola Marymount University in Los Angeles has also proved a helpful adviser to this project in its early stages.

I will always remember in a special way the late Nuba civil affairs administrator, Commander Mohamed Juma Nayel, for the warmth and candor of our interviews. For me, Juma embodied the spirit of the "free Nuba" during the war.

The journey this book seeks to represent, however, would never have been undertaken were it not for the constant encouragement, support and counsel of my friend Ron Austin, who has been the godfather of this endeavor from its inception during a discussion on a pier in Manhattan Beach in the late 1990s to the media campaigns on behalf of the Nuba to his role as first critic of the various forms this book has taken over the years.

The board of directors of the Windhover Forum, a Catholic educational and media organization over which Mr. Austin presides, has sustained this project, as well as the documentary *The Hidden Gift* in many ways, not least of all through fundraising. I wish to single out Michael Feeley, the Forum's legal counsel, for his advice and dedication.

Fine arts photographer Jim Nicholls has been my comrade-in-arms in many adventures (and misadventures) from Bosnia to Sudan. His images do far more than accompany this text; in many cases, they have inspired it.

I also wish to express my gratitude to other colleagues in the field, particularly David Tlapek, who directed *The Hidden Gift: War & Faith in Sudan,* and Peter Salapatas, the principal cinematographer for the documentary, in whose footage both the physical and moral beauty of the Nuba were captured.

I wish to acknowledge Sandra De Groot, project developer at William B. Eerdmans Publishing Company, in a special way for her unfailing commitment to this project, and for her patience.

Many others too numerous to name have aided and abetted the

completion of this book. Let me note the following: Jason Barreda, Betsy Bliss, James and Ellie Buchanan, Leah Buturain-Schneider, Elena Karina Byrne, Jim Carolla, Roxanne Christ, Stuart and Beverly Denenberg, Ed and Doris Eisenstein, Jack and Rosie Evans, Zak Forsman, Gordon Fuglie, Mary Ann Glendon, Rhett and Janice Gist, Eric Jessen, Joop Koopman, Chris Krause, Lucile and Walter Kuns, Lino Lauro, Francis X. Maier, Christopher Merrill, the law firm of Latham & Watkins, Laura Laurent, David and Malia Melvin, Nat Hentoff, David Rintels and Victoria Riskin, Jincks Rodger, Jean-Claude Sakoun and Gloria Sanchez, Rev. Anthony Scannell, Marc Seltzer and Christina Snyder, Ruth Seymour, Kevin Shah, Rabbis Scott and Jackie Shapiro, Patt and Jack Shea, Rt. Rev. Archimandrite Alexei Smith, Sarah Spitz, Doug and Earlene Thompson, Frank Thompson, and Paul Wolff.

None of the friends and colleagues mentioned in this acknowledgment bears the slightest responsibility for the book's shortcomings. These are mine alone.

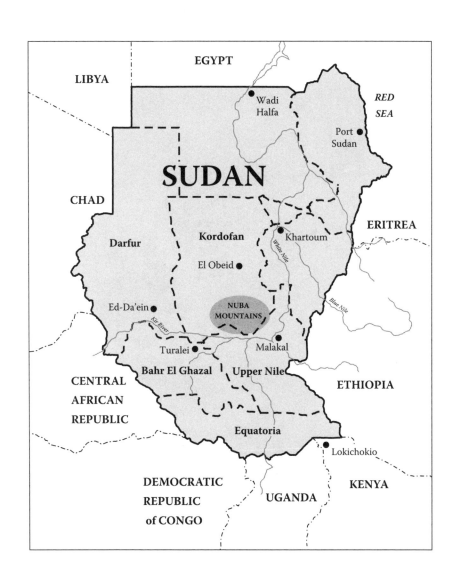

EGYPT

LIBYA

RED
SEA

Wadi
Halfa

Port
Sudan

CHAD

SUDAN

Darfur

Kordofan

Khartoum

ERITREA

El Obeid

White Nile

Ed-Da'ein

Kir River

NUBA
MOUNTAINS

Blue Nile

Turalei

Malakal

CENTRAL
AFRICAN
REPUBLIC

Bahr El Ghazal

Upper Nile

ETHIOPIA

Equatoria

Lokichokio

DEMOCRATIC
REPUBLIC
of CONGO

UGANDA

KENYA

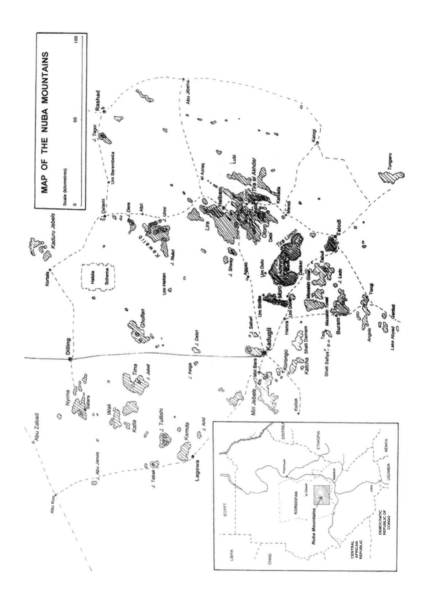

MAP OF THE NUBA MOUNTAINS

Scale (kilometres)

0   50   100

How the Nuba Came to Be

"On this mountain, which the people call Kumu Mountain, a woman was once ready to give birth. (In the beginning, people used to cut open the stomachs of women to get the child. They did not yet know how children were born.) The woman was on Kumu waiting to deliver, and they were sharpening the knives to take her child.

"Suddenly, a woman came from above, wearing proper clothes, all white and so on. And the woman from above said, 'Stop!' And they stopped, the ones who were prepared to cut her, the woman who had come to Kumu. They ran away in surprise.

"The heavenly woman then taught the mother how to get delivered of a child without knives, without killing. And the child was born. The woman on Kumu was surprised.

"And the men with knives came back to Kumu with food to offer the woman from above. And the woman from above said: 'Do you see? This is how humans come into the world. Not with knives and cutting.'

"This is how the Nuba came to be, when they stopped cutting the women."

A Nuba creation story told to the author,
December 24, 1998

Introduction

I have always believed that it is one of the functions of journalism to bring to light what is hidden, to tell not the story that everyone is telling, but the one that no one is, to seek out the "invisible" realities that, all too often, can't be seen from our customary vantage points and with our typical points of reference — victimizations that fall through the cracks of things, the very invisibility of which give their perpetrators a free hand.

That was my first reason for going to the remote Nuba Mountains of central Sudan, where a military junta had been conducting a ruthless war of liquidation against a civilian population for years with impunity.

The second reason for going, or, rather, for going *back*, had to do with something that I heard there.

It was, I think, my first interview, as it happened, with a commander of the insurgent forces of the Sudan People's Liberation Army (SPLA) in the Nuba Mountains. I knew that the SPLA's war against government troops in the region had bogged down and I had been told that they were looking for more sophisticated weapons systems to fight Khartoum's bombers — "stinger" missiles, for example, from discreet U.S. suppliers. I asked the young commander a question that I thought might launch us into that discussion.

"So, what's the most important thing your soldiers need out here in the Nuba Mountains?" I said, getting my notebook out.

"The *most* important thing?" he asked back through translators, with a wistfulness I hadn't expected from a military man. "The most important thing my soldiers need," he said, "is to learn to fight and not to hate."

I looked up. Not unfamiliar with "popular" militias and guerilla movements from both the Israeli-Palestinian conflict and from the Balkan War, it was the last thing I expected to hear.

"Fight the enemy, if you must," he went on, "but why catch his disease?"

(For good measure, he thought the "stinger" missiles a splendid idea when I brought it up later. To my knowledge, he never got them.)

As I was to discover, the soldier's remark proved to be characteristic of a Nuba approach to struggle, and, coupled with their history of tribal and religious tolerance, hinted at a farsightedness that stood in stark contrast with much of Sudanese history, and even with attitudes that I had found in other corners of the insurgency.

It was more than farsightedness, though. There was a spirituality hidden in the heart of the Nuba experience, one sensed, a complex, double-edged ethos, both determined and generous, that had made such sagacity possible.

"I will build my civilization," the late Nuba political leader Yusuf Kuwa once wrote of his aims, "and then I will forgive everyone who humiliated me."

*   *   *

Humanitarian Roger Winter once noted in an article he wrote on the Nuba Mountains that "being neither a Sudan historian nor anthropologist, [the scholarly and historical data] is entirely drawn from others. . . . I only seek to provide a framework with which to understand my own experiences."[1]

A similar disclaimer is in order here. I experienced the Nuba Mountains long before I knew very much about them. This is not a old Sudan hand's or expert's book on what one can only hope is the recently concluded twenty-two-year Sudanese civil war between government forces and insurgent armies in southern and central Sudan.

Still less does it speak for the Nuba. Thankfully, their isolation now ended, they are beginning to speak for themselves. As a Nuba priest, Father Butros Trille, told me on my last visit in 2004: "Before, in the time of [anthropologist Siegfried] Nadel and [photographer Leni] Riefenstahl, we were the silent Nuba, whose languages no outsider spoke, and who hadn't the education to respond to western questions. Now the silent Nuba are beginning to speak."

War and Faith in Sudan is a very personal enterprise: essays and photographs drawn from six trips photographer Jim Nicholls and I made to the Nuba Mountains in central Sudan and northern Bahr al-Ghazal during the last years of the civil war, from 1998-2001, and capped by a return trip to the region in December 2004 as the last touches were being applied to the peace agreement signed by the Government of Sudan and the Sudan People's Liberation Movement (SPLM) on January 9, 2005.

The reportage is amplified by journal notes, further research, and, of course, by the intimations that only memory affords. As Eudora Welty has written:

"I found the world out there revealing because . . . *memory* had become attached to seeing."

The regime that persecuted the Nuba relied, above all, on the hope that the "disappearance" of these remote and isolated peoples would go unnoticed. This account, in its own small way, seeks to honor the dead by defying that hope.

*   *   *

Since the focus of this book is the Nuba Mountains during the last phase of the government of Sudan's "war against the Nuba," which it prosecuted as part of its broader struggle with southern insurgents, it's perhaps useful at the outset to sketch some of the historical background of the war.

The Nuba people are one of Africa's most remarkable indigenous cultures. At once irenic and fiercely loyal to their way of life, the Nuba burst on to the modern historical stage with their resistance to Turko-

Egyptian ruler Mohamed Ali's military forays into *bilad al-Sudan,* "land of the blacks," for gold and slaves in 1821.

Nuba origins are still a matter of dispute.

As S. F. Nadel, the British anthropologist who compiled an exhaustive study of the Nuba, wrote laconically of his attempts to piece together an account of Nuba origins from fieldwork, "The traditions and memories of the people yield sparse information. . . . In some tribes the tradition of past movements or previous places of settlement are summarized in one sentence: 'We have always lived here.'"[2]

Even the very word "Nuba" is not indigenous, but likely a generic term used by Egyptians and other Nile dwellers to characterize the black peoples of the Sudanese interior, traditional targets of their slave raids.[3]

The Nuba, based in southern Kordofan in central Sudan, are often confused with *Nubians,* members of a quite different — though some argue related — culture centered in the lower Nile Valley. The best that can be said is that the available evidence doesn't allow the nature of the relationship between "hill Nuba" and Nilotic Nubians, if any, to be definitively settled.

What suggests connections to some but by no means all scholars are linguistic affinities between classical Nubian and the vocabularies of some Nuba tribes and the possibility of Nubian Christian ritual remnants in the religious practices of certain Nuba communities.[4]

What can be surmised from history is that the Nuba were probably the indigenous population of much of what we now call northern Sudan, but that they, under pressure from advancing Arab tribes, retreated over a period of centuries to defensive positions in the mountains.

As H. A. MacMichael writes,

"In the earliest days and for thousands of subsequent years the ancestors of the Nuba probably held the greater part of this country (i.e., what is known as Kordofan), except the northernmost deserts. Beaten back by other races that ruled the Nile banks in successive generations, by tribes from the interior, and finally by the nomad Arabs, the Nuba have now retired to the mountains of southern Kordofan."[5]

While Nuba have historically tended to organize themselves in loose settlements governed largely by custom and consent rather than by tribal chieftains, the powerful kingdom of Tegali, founded in the extreme northeast part of the Nuba Mountains in the sixteenth century, with its dynastic kings, is an exception. Significantly, it was through the Tegali kingdom, with its links to Muslim centers in northern Sudan, that Islam first came to the Nuba Mountains, although, in a typically Nuba way, the new faith neither precipitated a religious crisis, nor were the powerful Tegali rulers able to compromise the local autonomy of Nuba tribes.

However, by the nineteenth century, with the Tegali kingdom in decline, the Nuba found themselves, along with the Dinka to the south, the particular focus of predatory slave raids. These raids were widespread during the *Turkiyya,* the Turkish rule of Sudan that began with the Turko-Egyptian conquest in 1821.

At the same time, nomadic Arab tribes called the *Baggara,*[6] which had previously confined themselves to the plains of Kordofan and Darfur, migrated into the valleys of the Nuba Mountains in search of water and pasture for their herds, driving the Nuba off their best agricultural land and into the hills. Not incidentally, the Baggara were not averse to conducting their own slave raids against Nuba communities.

Eventually, a kind of *modus vivendi,* based on barter and trade, developed between Nuba and Baggara, though not without sporadic intercommunity violence.

The advent of the *Mahdia,* the late nineteenth-century popular revolt against Egyptian rule in Sudan, proved still more devastating to the peoples of the mountain. Initially supportive of the uprising because of its opposition to Turko-Egyptian slave raiding, some Nuba tribes refused to submit to the Mahdist state (1881-98), which also demanded its tribute of slaves, provoking swift government retaliation. Khartoum proved unable to crush Nuba resistance, though destruction and loss of life were widespread.

The British administration of Sudan (1899-1955) fared little better: thirty uprisings and rebellions — including two large-scale revolts and prolonged resistance efforts — took place against British government policy in the Nuba Mountains between 1900 and 1945. Nuba discontent had its roots in Britain's incoherent and shifting policies toward African tribal cultures, an incoherence that revolved around the Closed Districts Ordinance of 1922, which effectively isolated the Nuba Mountains and southern Sudan from northern Arab influence. "The British," notes one report, "never resolved the dilemma of whether the Nuba as a whole should be 'preserved' and isolated from Arab influence, or assimilated (on unequal terms) with the North."[7]

Meanwhile, Khartoum, in a pattern that was to prove enduring, sought to promote "indirect rule" in the restive Nuba Mountains by recruiting chiefs and community leaders to do the government's bidding — "Nuba 'friendlies' to pacify the rebels."[8]

Sudanese independence in 1956 only accelerated the pace of change, along with the marginalization of the Nuba and other ethnic African communities throughout the country. Lack of economic opportunity forced many Nuba men to migrate to northern towns. There they found low-paying work as agricultural laborers, servants, and soldiers.

In the mountains themselves, the central government's campaign of "Sudanization," meaning the imposition of northern Arabic and Islamic cultural and religious norms on the country's traditional tribal cultures, was vigorously enforced, sometimes with violence.

As historian R. S. O'Fahey writes, "The present regime, like the British in the second *Turkiyya*, seeks to be inclusive, but inclusive by a process based on the premise of obliterating all identities other than that which it has constructed for itself. . . . The very fragility of the Sudanese state reinforces the savagery with which it attempts to assert its survival."[9] The various forms of resistance to that policy has meant that Sudan has known only eleven years of relative peace since 1956.

The Nuba, conscious of their vulnerable geographical position at Sudan's cultural epicenter, sat out the first of Sudan's two southern-generated civil wars (1955-1972). In fact, many Nuba served in the northern military that fought the southern insurgents, a "detail" which many older southerners have not forgotten. By the mid-1980s, however, northern Arab elites, eager to develop Arab-owned agribusinesses, had begun to push Nuba farmers out of their fertile valleys. As a result of these government policies, tens of thousands of Nuba died in the famines of the late 1980s and early '90s.

But worse was yet to come.

In June 1989, an Islamist junta, under the leadership of General Omar Hassan Ahmed al-Bashir, seized power in Khartoum from the indecisive but legitimately elected government of Sadiq al-Mahdi — a government that appeared on the verge of settling the then-six-year-old civil war with the South.

(I prefer to employ the term "Islamist" rather than "Islamic" or "Islamic fundamentalist" for reasons of clarity. Islamist implies adherence to a political and revolutionary ideology, often utopian in characters, employing the language of Islamic revivalism and aimed at the seizure of state power.)

The ideological leader of the coup was the University of London and Sorbonne-educated founder of the Sudanese Muslim Brotherhood, Hasan al-Turabi (b. 1932).[10] The culmination of a long process of infiltration and political horse-trading, the National Islamic Front's (NIF) victory signaled a dramatic escalation of the intensity and scope of the civil war.

As Mohamed Mahmoud has written, "In justifying its existence and trying to invest itself with legitimacy, the regime made the conflict in the South its rallying cry. The conflict was immediately 'Islamized' and thrust upon the Northern public imagination as a 'jihad.'"[11] By the early 1990s, SPLA military and recruitment successes in the Nuba Mountains had opened a new front in the war, pressing the conflict into northern Sudan itself, a threat to which Khartoum responded with all the violence at its command.

CHAPTER 1

Reading Rilke in the Nuba Mountains

"More and more in my life and in my work I am guided by the effort to correct our old repressions, which have removed and gradually estranged from us the mysteries out of whose abundance our lives might become truly infinite. It is true that these mysteries are dreadful, and people have always drawn away from them. But where can we find anything sweet and glorious that would never wear *this* mask, the mask of the dreadful? Life — and we know nothing else — , isn't Life itself dreadful? But as soon as we acknowledge its dreadfulness (not as opponents: what kind of match could we be for it?), but somehow with a confidence that this very dreadfulness may be something completely *ours,* though something that is just now too great, too vast, too incomprehensible for our learning hearts — : as soon as we accept Life's most terrifying dreadfulness, at the risk of perishing from it (i.e., from our own Too-much!) — : then an intuition of blessedness will open up for us, and at this cost, will be ours. Whoever does not, sometime or other, give his full consent, his full and *joyous* consent, to the dreadfulness of life, can never take possession of the unutterable abundance and power of our existence; can only walk on its edge, and one day, when the judgment is given, will have been neither alive nor dead."

Rainer Maria Rilke[1]

Arrival of a relief plane, Nuba Mountains

The Antonov troop carrier skidded onto the sandy tarmac of the airstrip in a cloud of dust, fishtailing its way to a halt in the bush clearing known on military maps as Charlie-5.

It had been an eventful landing.

The Russian-made plane, Afghan War vintage certainly, was packed to the rafters with relief supplies for the beleaguered Nuba people of central Sudan — not the least of these provisions, strapped in amidst the cargo, an exiled Sudanese bishop paying his semi-annual visit to frontline parishes, a missionary priest, a Nuba relief coordinator, Washington, D.C.-based human rights activists, a journalist (yours truly), and the Greek-born cameraman, who, not incidentally, had been hounding me for weeks about whether we were going to a war zone.

Peter Salapatas, the cinematographer, had done a stint on the Turkish border with the Greek Army, and knew enough to be nervous.

Don't worry, I had told him at our first planning meeting. In conversations with the bishop, I had been assured that, while there were the inevitable risks, the area we were visiting in the Nuba Mountains had been "pacified." His word.

And a fairly creative use of the word it was, too — a fact that became increasingly apparent as the trip to the Nuba Mountains unfolded.

There was the incident at the airport in Lokichokio on the Kenya-Sudan border, launching pad for major relief operations in southern Sudan, and, more discreetly, for flights that the Khartoum government had not approved, "illegal" flights, like ours, into areas the regime had declared off limits to foreigners.

A few of us had drifted over to an Aussie bush pilot on the tarmac, "Quig" by name, just back from a relief run over southern Sudan, to quiz him on "conditions."

We had been told by the bishop to be wary of strangers in transit, since practically everything in a place like Lokichokio has ears.

"No problem," the pilot answered, genially. "You're okay as long as you're not going to the Nuba Mountains. Some big offensive."

And then there were the sullen Russian pilots of the Antonov-32 we ended up piling into, unflappable veterans of these high-risk commutes, who, nevertheless, felt the need to pass around a bottle of vodka as part of crew preparations before the craft shuddered into the skies for the three-hour flight to central Sudan.

The final indication that "pacified" might not be the most accurate word to describe the terrain we were entering came when artillery shells and the crackle of small arms fire accompanied our plane's sudden and precipitous descent to the landing strip in the Nuba Mountains.

"Peter, get away from the window," I said to the cinematographer who had his eyes glued to the glass.

"What?"

"That's gunfire, get away from the window," I repeated, getting into my best war correspondent's mode.

"We *are* in a war zone!" Peter declared.

"You know what?" I said, bracing myself for the landing of a lifetime. "You're right."

*   *   *

How I came to find myself in a situation like this, one of the few journalists (until recently) to venture into the Nuba Mountains, isn't altogether easy to explain. In my case, the ingredients included one unseasonably balmy southern California night, the Manhattan Beach pier, a good dinner, several cigars, and a close friend who is fond of getting me into trouble. Add a serious discussion of the war in Sudan, an offer to do a story, and you're halfway there.

"You're going," was my friend's conclusion as we shook hands that night. "I don't know how we're going to get you there, but you're going."

Actually, Sudan had been a mysterious presence in my life, my imaginative life, at least, for years — though, pierside conversations aside, I had never had any particular ambitions to go there.

While living in Jerusalem in the 1980s, and writing as a correspondent for a U.S.-based Catholic newspaper, I had stumbled on the work of the Sudanese writer Tayeb Salih (b. 1929), especially his novel *Season of Migration to the North,* now considered a classic of the African literary canon in Arabic.

I had been sitting in a Palestinian café in East Jerusalem playing

14

cards with friends when an Armenian schoolteacher at another table came over to ask, out of the blue, whether I had read Tayeb Salih. When I shook my head, he leaned over, with a slightly conspiratorial air, to whisper that I would never understand the dilemma of a mutual friend, a Palestinian-American who had returned to the city to take over his late father's business affairs, until I had.

It was good advice, and not only in terms of my friend Bassem's problems. The Sudanese writer has created an almost clinical study of the psychology of cultural dislocation, the often-violent contradictions modernity inevitably, and with the best intentions, introduces into traditional societies. Written in 1967, *Season of Migration to the North* evokes a landscape of permanent exile, the existential features of a world in which no one can go home again.

The book's narrator, a village-born but British-educated Sudanese, working as an Education Ministry bureaucrat, is haunted by the apparent suicide of an older villager, like him an Oxford graduate, who had returned, mysteriously, to the simplicities of rural life.

In one of the novel's most gripping passages, the narrator attempts to drown his own contradictions in the waters of the Nile. As he swims further into the river currents, he finds that he is poised halfway between north and south, "unable to continue, and unable to return."[2]

The plight of the Nubians of Wadi Halfa in southern Egypt and northern Sudan, victims of the massive Aswan Dam project of the 1960s, had also etched itself in my mind — an image also of loss.[3] For the Aswan Dam, often referred to by critics as "Nasser's Pyramid," necessitated the destruction of the historic heartland of Nubian culture.

Nubian singer Hamza el-Din's song "Escalay — The Water Wheel," famously captures, with its thumping rhythms and bobbing, free-form melody, the essence of this modern tragedy in the image of a boy tending the ox-driven waterwheels that used to irrigate fields along the banks of the Nile — a millennial river civilization buried forever under the waters of the High Dam.

Alan Moorehead, in his account of early nineteenth-century explorations of Wadi Halfa, describes it as "one of the most beautiful parts of the river... Hundreds of water wheels pumped life into the sand, and on either bank fertile crops and forests of mimosas and acacias spread

away. Wild thyme grew on the many green islands in the river, and water birds in thousands were constantly lighting down to feed or passing
overhead."[4]

As el-Din himself has written of the circumstances of the composi-
tion of "Escalay": "When I went back and saw my village and my people
in a different place [in the resettlement after the completion of the
dam], I saw in their eyes the loss. I saw my people were lost. They had
moved to an almost semi-desert place. When I came back I was lost myself. I was playing my *oud* [a classical Arabic stringed instrument], doing nothing but repeating a phrase. "[5]

The Nuba, too, were at least a file card in my mind before I found
myself unexpectedly their guest, mainly through the well-known photographs Leni Riefenstahl took of them in the 1960s and '70s. Actually, I
am not sure I'd ever seen the photographs themselves before I found
them in a Nairobi bookshop *after* I had returned from the Nuba Mountains, but I had heard that Riefenstahl, the creator of such Nazi-inspired
film classics as *Triumph of the Will* and *Olympia,* had found, apparently, in the Nuba people of Sudan, the realization of her arcadian
dreams — a proud, beautiful people, unspoiled by western civilization,
living, as she saw it, in a Rousseauian state of unencumbered innocence
and sensuality.

But Sudan did not come definitively into my life, into focus as it
were, until 1997, when, while working as a freelance writer in Los Angeles, friends urged me to interview a Sudanese bishop who was visiting
Washington, D.C., looking for media exposure. The dynamic, sixtyish
Bishop Macram Max Gassis is the Roman Catholic bishop of El Obeid
Diocese in central Sudan, a sprawling ecclesiastical jurisdiction, twice
the size of Italy, which includes the Nuba Mountains. The plight of
Christian and other religious minorities in the Muslim world has been a
key concern since I began writing for newspapers in the mid-1980s, but
it was the Nuba angle that particularly caught my attention.

The bishop proved to be an engaging and persuasive interview, just
the sort journalists warm to — passionate, dramatic, straightforward,
and, most importantly, indiscreet.

There was never any diplomatic hedging, for example, when the
subject was the National Islamic Front (NIF) regime in Khartoum:

If we say that communism is bad, I think that Islamic fundamentalism is even more dangerous. [Sudanese Islamist ideologue] Hasan al-Turabi's movement [the basis of the NIF] is not only religious, but a kind of political and economic ideology as well. Al-Turabi says: We [the third world] have tried capitalism, and it failed; socialism, it failed, too. Now it's the time for Islam. That's his agenda: that his brand of Islamic ideology should spread through the whole of Africa. Terrorism, torture — anything that allows them to reach their goals is justified.

When asked what measures the Khartoum government had taken against the people in his diocese, he shot back,

What *measures?* Well, for starters, they've denied access to non-governmental organizations (NGOs) seeking to help the Nuba, they've held up relief supplies, lifesaving medicines, and development aid to the Nuba Mountains. In fact, they've enforced a kind of total isolation. The only presence, the only voice the Nuba people have in Europe and America is the Church. [As] for the international community, [it] started paying attention to the plight of the Nuba people only about five years ago [in 1992], and, to date, Khartoum has vetoed World Food Program assistance or help from UNICEF for the Nuba.

Summarizing his position nicely, he declared,

Listen, fortunately I don't have to sugarcoat my words when I speak of these things. I'm not a politician. . . They [the Khartoum government] really want to annihilate these people.

Born in Khartoum, Sudan's capital, in 1938, Macram Max Gassis grew up in a prosperous household, his family lineage the classic northern Sudanese mix of Syrian, Somali, Darfuri, and Egyptian (Coptic) backgrounds. Raised as a Catholic, he overcame his evangelical mother's objections and enrolled in the seminary, doing his studies in Verona, Italy, and in England under the auspices of the Comboni Missionary Fathers, an Italian religious congregation devoted to African missions, returning to Sudan as a parish priest in 1964. By 1968, he was chancellor of the Khartoum Archdiocese, and five years later, began a long stint as secretary-general of the Sudanese Bishops' Conference. In the late 1970s, Gassis went to the United States to study canon law and administration at Washington, D.C.'s prestigious Catholic University of America. Father Gassis was already involved in relief work as chairman of SudanAid (Caritas Sudan) in the early 1980s, and, after five years as apostolic administrator of the El Obeid Diocese in central Sudan (the see of St. Daniel Comboni, father of Catholic missions in Africa, and historic seat of more than a century of Catholic missionary activity in the country) he was consecrated as its bishop in 1988.

The new bishop, the only native Arabic-speaker among the Sudanese hierarchy, most of whom hail from Christian-dominated southern Sudan or from Italy, acted as liaison between the bishops and the government until he was placed under criminal indictment by the authorities for criticizing Sudan's human rights record abroad. Failing to persuade the government of President Sadiq al-Mahdi to take responsibility for massacres by government-armed tribesmen in south-central Sudan (more than a thousand Dinka men, women, and children were killed and burnt to death by government-armed Rizegat tribesmen in El-Da'en, a town in southern Darfur, on March 27-28, 1987), Gassis, against the advice of some church officials, testified before a committee of the U.S. Congress in 1988, and denounced the Sudanese government.

Two years later, Gassis was diagnosed with cancer and went to the United States for treatment. While there, two developments occurred which determined the future course of events. First, in June 1989, the National Islamic Front, a coalition of Islamist groups, allied with elements in the military, seized power from a weak but popularly elected government. Under the al-Mahdi administration, Gassis had been confident that his conviction would eventually be overturned. Given the radical tenor of the new NIF regime, however, that hope was dashed. And then, while still abroad, he was warned privately, through church contacts in the Sudanese military, that his safety could not be guaranteed, that he should not return to his diocese. In the absence of a resi-

Bishop Gassis en route to Turalei, northern Bahr al-Ghazal

dent bishop, the Vatican appointed an apostolic administrator in El Obeid to manage diocesan affairs.

Faced with what amounted to exile, and with the civil war again in high gear, Gassis soon realized that his peripatetic situation placed him in a unique position to speak out on issues and to alert the world to the sufferings of Christians and other marginalized peoples in his war-torn country. Throughout the 1990s, Gassis traveled tirelessly, briefing bishops' conferences, government officials, non-government agencies and the media about conditions in Sudan. By mid-decade, he had testified before Congress, addressed the European Parliament in Brussels, testified before the United Nations Human Rights Commission in Geneva on numerous occasions, and met with then-U.N. Secretary-General Boutros Boutros-Ghali.

In the late 1990s, through the efforts of politically well-connected associates in Washington, Gassis became a familiar presence on Capitol Hill and at the State Department, and an influence on the formulation of U.S. Sudan policy in both the Clinton and Bush administrations. The eminent Sudanese scholar Francis Deng said of Gassis during testimony before the U.S. Commission on International Religious Freedom in 2000, "This man has done a tremendous job in transcending the keen divisions within [his] country. You look at him, and normally he would be considered a northern Sudanese, and by normal words of identity he would be called an Arab. It is a question of a man leaving the privileged category to identify with the underdog."[6]

Eventually reestablishing himself in Nairobi, Kenya, Bishop Gassis learned in August 1995, through Christian Solidarity International (CSI) workers in southern Sudan,[7] that there was an air corridor to the Nuba Mountains, that it was possible, though risky, to fly, in defiance of government edicts, to SPLA-controlled zones in his central Sudanese diocese. (Military authorities routinely threatened to attack or intercept unauthorized flights to the Nuba Mountains.) With the diocese effectively split in two — the northern sector under government control (and an apostolic administrator), and the southern part of the diocese, which included the Nuba Mountains, under the SPLA — the bishop realized that he could return to pastoral work in the rebel-held territories to which he did have access, and to building up Church and civilian life among the long-suffering Nuba.

"It's ironic, isn't it?" the bishop said later. "In the old days, before the war, the isolation, the lack of roads, made it almost impossible to reach these people. Now, because of the war, the Nuba are the only ones we can reach."

At the close of the interview, he lamented, a bit slyly, I thought, that the risks of flying into the Nuba Mountains kept so many journalists from covering the situation, and wondered, since I'd had war experience, if I would ever consider accompanying him on one of his pastoral visits.

Intrigued by the prospect of writing about the fabled Nuba, I said yes, of course; but, frankly, thought it unlikely that I would ever hear from Gassis again. And I didn't until one day in late November, a year since I had spoken to the bishop, I heard that slightly peeved voice on the other end of the line, saying, with only the briefest formalities, "Gabriel, we're leaving on the 21st for the Nuba Mountains; when are you coming?"

*   *   *

The belly of the Antonov groaned open to reveal a large dusty clearing in the African bush. It was already mid-afternoon and temperatures hovered in the low nineties. The delays in Lokichokio — misweighted provisions, a change of planes — had cost us precious hours and the Russian crew was rattled, eager to discharge its cargo and return to the relative safety of the skies.

On subsequent trips to the region, I found the Russians only marginally friendlier. I once asked the pilot, Alexander, how an old Soviet troop carrier ended up in Kenya. "We flew it here from an air base in the Urals," he said matter-of-factly, turning his back to me. Something in his attitude suggested that I should stop asking questions.

The world of the Nuba Mountains was little more than a hard glare from the hold of the plane at first. But we could clearly make out Nuba porters, fifty or so, from nearby villages that had assembled in rows to ferry our supplies across the mountains. They stood silently, away from the plane, at perfect attention.

Accustomed to scenes of rural children mobbing visitors, I found the stillness a little uncanny.

I recalled what the bishop had said in that first interview: "The Nuba are a very disciplined people. When the British ruled Sudan, they said that the Nuba make good soldiers, that they are disciplined by nature."

I later learned that the porters hailed from a tribe living in the vicinity of the airstrip that, since the SPLA had cleared it in the mid-90s, had made ferrying supplies something of a local monopoly. They had paid for it, though, in frequent aerial attacks on their villages due to their proximity to a military asset.

We could also make out, on the edge of the airstrip, the carcass of a cargo plane that, apparently, had managed an even rougher landing than we. Overshooting the end of the airstrip, the small Antonov had tumbled through trees and scrub brush until it came to rest nose down in a gully, its propellers sheared off. According to the bishop, the plane had been gun running for rebel units in the area. Nuba soldiers, in the process of stripping the plane for parts, had coated the fuselage with mud to disguise it from the air — an ineffective ruse, one would have thought, given that the plane's upended tail towered above the trees.

"Welcome to the ninth century," I said to myself as I prepared to scuttle down the long ramp onto terrain as unfamiliar as a lunar landscape. It was clear from the first that we had landed in a very different place from any we westerners knew. My work had taken me in the past to some remote locales, rural upper Egypt for example, and one of the American human rights activists on board, Sharon Payt, who worked for U.S. Senator Sam Brownback, had spent time in Afghanistan. But this was stranger still: It was as if we had been deposited in another age, in a different consciousness.

Until now, in our journey, even in the developing countries through which we had passed, with their counterpoint of ancient and modern improvisations, we still had had the reassuring presence of the cultural markers of our own civilization: the infrastructures of airports, vehicles, highways, communications networks, electricity that define not only the physical landscape of the modern world, but, more importantly, its psychic one: the illusions of control, and the even greater illusions of safety.

There were no such markers here in this environment of nearly incomparable isolation — without roads, vehicles and electricity, and regionally, except for Heiban, Talodi, Dilling and Kadugli, none of which we would be visiting, nothing that could even remotely be called a town. We were, quite simply, hundreds of miles from anything we understood, in another world, one whose hardships were compounded by war, that, were it not for the skill and benevolence of our guides, along with reasonable luck with enemy militias and land mines, we would not, and could not survive.

As I would later warn travelers to the area, "Read all you want, and by all means, get into the best physical shape of your life, but there is nothing that adequately prepares a westerner for the Nuba Mountains."

The bishop, leader of our expedition, having greeted a uniformed representative of the Sudan People's Liberation Movement, the *de facto* "government" in these hills, was the first to leap into the small crowd of Nuba leaders, catechists, Catholic lay leaders, clergy, and soldiers who only now approached the plane.

Founded in 1983, in the wake of the promulgation of then-Sudanese president Jafaar Nimeiri's infamous "September Laws,"[8] the Sudan People's Liberation Army (SPLA), and its political wing, the Sudan People's Liberation Movement (SPLM), launched the second, and, to date, longer, of two historic insurgencies of southern and now central Sudanese peoples against the cultural, religious, and economic hegemony of Khartoum.

Originally confined to southern Sudanese provinces, by the mid-1980s, the rebellion had spread to the Nuba Mountains. In 1992, at the peak of government assaults on the region, Nuba in rebel-held areas persuaded the SPLA leadership to establish a full array of civilian institutions, creating what the humanitarian organization African Rights has called "an unprecedented political renaissance" in non-government held areas of the Nuba Mountains.[9]

Peter, the cameraman, was already out filming everything in sight, although I had advised him not to venture toward the still-unmoving Nuba villagers at the airstrip's edge until we knew what the protocol was.

I couldn't take my eyes off them, the Nuba at the edge of the airstrip. When I had imagined how things would be in the few harried weeks between the bishop's invitation and our arrival, Chiapas, rural southern Mexico, I now realized, had been my unconscious model: tall tropical forests, muddy roads, Nuba elders in linen caftans, refugees sleeping on the earthen floors of small lime-washed chapels. (I had spent some time covering the ethnic strife in Chiapas for a Catholic newspaper earlier that year.)

The poverty that greeted us on the airstrip was of an altogether different order. At some distance from the plane, a few Nuba men, along with many women and adolescents, stood in straight rows at an easy attention in the hot sun, grouped, one assumed, in families, awaiting word that they might join the parade of porters unloading supplies.

Silent, barefoot, lean. The Nuba, only a generation ago, had been celebrated for their physical prowess and robust physiques, for the wrestling matches that were the centerpieces of their seasonal celebrations. Now, clothed in tatters — dusty khakis, torn t-shirts, shreds of old sweaters — their bodies weakened by the diseases and malnutrition that have become a way of life since attacks on the Nuba began more than a decade ago, they had the gaunt look of prisoners of war.

Writer Ian Fisher, who paid a visit to the Nuba Mountains for the *New York Times* in 2001, described the Nuba he saw as "scarecrows," as if "their clothes simply eroded from their bodies."[10]

A far cry, I could not help thinking, from earlier first encounters with the Nuba: Leni Riefenstahl's gentle Mesakin Nuba giants who led her by the hand into their villages, or photojournalist George Rodger's account of an early photo shoot among the Korongo, a Nuba tribe in the western *jebels*:[11]

> Of tremendous stature and physique, bullet-headed and beetle-browed, the tribesmen appear fierce and warlike; but they are peaceful . . . good natured, easy-going. . . . All of them carried javelins with polished blades and wore little amulets of animal hide tied around their necks or massive biceps.[12]

And yet, even on this first encounter, it was not hard to notice something other than deprivation. It was chiefly in the stance, I thought, the way the Nuba looked you in the eye, the straight, almost military posture, the quiet indomitability of people who have seen the worst, and survived, the gentle, yet steely quality of their reserve.

I was not looking at a defeated people.

In fact, as humanitarian activist Roger Winter pointed out in a 1996 article he published on the Nuba crisis, the unprecedented military isolation of the Nuba Mountains had, paradoxically, forced the people into "an uncommon pattern of self-reliance, [and that] that self-reliance, coupled with an empowering pride," had produced a deep popular spirit in the free Nuba. "That some Nuba survive free," he concluded, "has nothing to do with the international community," but is due "entirely to their own efforts," their own ingenious solidarity.[13]

They would need those inner resources.

The effect of Sudan's long civil war on the Nuba, as well as on other mainly southern and central Sudanese peoples, had been nothing less than catastrophic.

According to the 1983 census, the population of Nuba districts totaled more than a million, nearly five percent of the total population of Sudan, before war engulfed the region in the early 1990s.

While precise numbers have always been hard to come by, and will be for some time, Neroun Phillip, a Nuba, and executive director of the Nuba Relief, Rehabilitation and Development Organization (NRRDO), a Nairobi, Kenya-based relief agency, told me in 1998, that out of a prewar population of two million, not more than 500,000 Nuba, at most, still clung to a precarious life in these hills. The rest had either perished or been internally displaced in the years of grueling civil war.

African Rights estimated in the mid-1990s that 200,000 Nuba resided in rebel-held territories, with perhaps a million Nuba under government control.[14]

A late twentieth-century report published by the U.S. Committee for Refugees tells a similar story. According to Millard Burr, author of the report, out of a population of 1.3 million, more than 200,000 Nuba perished in the years 1989-2001, when the first cease-fire was declared. The overall Sudanese war-related death toll for those years is more than 2.5 million, with more than four million displaced, mainly in the south.

"The Nuba who have been lost through acculturation, deracination, and the results of 'ethnic cleansing,'" Burr's report concludes, "can only be guessed at."[15]

"*Achillo,*" the bishop said in Tira, one of fifty indigenous languages and dialects spoken in the region, placing his outstretched hand on the bare shoulder of a Nuba tribesman in the traditional salute.

Many of those who approached the bishop on the tarmac had had to walk for days, often through hostile, government-held territories.

In those years, for the Nuba, Gassis was one of only a handful of "outsiders" who were willing to defy Khartoum's military embargoes on rebel-held zones in the Nuba Mountains. With the bishop came much-needed relief supplies, emergency rations of sorghum, salt, seed, agricultural tools, medicines, building materials, and, most importantly, personnel — clergy, medics, teachers to help build as much of a civilian infrastructure as war conditions allowed. But, more than that, he brought vital access to the outside world.

International aid agencies had been active until 1991, when Khartoum summarily expelled foreign relief workers from the Nuba Mountains and later declared rebel-held areas off limits to all foreign humanitarian operations.

Not surprisingly, the relief embargoes coincided with the onset of Khartoum's full-scale military operations in the Nuba Mountains, which, especially in the early 1990s, resulted in the death and displacement of tens of thousands of Nuba.

Lieutenant Khalid Abdel Karim Salih, a security officer in South Kordofan, who defected to the West in 1993, told a press conference in Switzerland that, by the early 1990s, at least 60,000-70,000 Nuba had been killed in government military operations — brutal campaigns virtually invisible to the outside world.[16]

A few journalists, notably the British freelance writer Julie Flint and photographer David Stewart Smith braved war conditions in 1995 to document atrocities in the Nuba Mountains. Later that year, Flint made the first major documentary on the Nuba's plight, entitled *Sudan's Secret War: The Nuba,* and returned to the region regularly after that.[17]

That same year, the London-based African Rights also managed to do the first full-scale investigation of human rights abuses in the Nuba Mountains. *Facing Genocide: The Nuba of Sudan,* which reported its findings, was published in 1995.[18]

The Nuba Relief, Rehabilitation, and Development Organization, founded in 1996, was also active to a limited degree in both relief and media arenas, the latter represented by the London-based Nuba affairs magazine *Nafir.* Neroun Phillip, NRRDO's executive director, a Nuba with a degree in economics from the University of Gezira, was a part of the bishop's team on this visit.

Still, it's safe to say that Gassis mounted the first, and, finally, most extensive outside effort in the midst of the war to address the ongoing needs of the Nuba, everything from health and education to water projects and agriculture — this, in addition, to establishing Catholic parishes — thereby strengthening their ability to resist.

As Abdel Aziz el-Hilu, current SPLA governor of South Kordofan, remarked in a speech to a U.S. church delegation to the Nuba Mountains in 2001:

> It is worth mentioning that during those difficult days when the Nuba were struggling against the regime that is waging a genocidal war against them, and the forces of nature, of famine and disease on the other side, the Catholic Church, under his lordship Bishop Macram Max took the initiative and the risk to make the first visit by a humanitarian body to the area in 1995. The visit had great impact on the morale of the people and gave hope to the persecuted and oppressed in the Nuba Mountains.[19]

I, too, milled among the Nuba dignitaries and priests around the plane, gingerly using the two words of Tira I had memorized en route, and the basic colloquial Arabic I'd picked up in the Middle East only to find that my Palestinian pronunciation, along with generous mistakes in grammar, rendered most of what I said unintelligible, even though a local Nuba-Arabic had long been the lingua franca in these mountains.

*   *   *

"Gabriel, you'd better be going now. The planes bomb around this time," the bishop warned as he sped off with one of his priests down the footpath leading into the hills on the diocese's one operational motorbike.

(It did not escape our notice that the good bishop had gone off with a wave, leaving the rest of us to the tender mercies of a trek to god-knew-where in the full heat of the day.)

"The planes bomb around this time": Eventually, you factor it in, like the weather.

I remember telephoning a friend in Nicaragua during that country's civil war. In the middle of the conversation, I was startled to hear a loud explosion. "Carlos, are you okay?" I shouted. "No problem," my friend replied evenly, "it's just the eight o'clock bomb."

A column quickly formed at the edge of the airstrip amid a small chorus of uncertainties. We had only the vaguest notion of where we were headed — a compound in the mountains, the name of which, like the airstrip, we were told never to mention.

"They know we're in the area," the bishop had briefed us in his Nairobi dining room, over passion fruit, the night before departure. "But they don't know where, exactly." The "they" were government troops stationed at garrisons interspersed with rebel positions throughout the area. It's safe to say that until you're on the ground you have no appreciation of just how closely intertwined combatants can be.

During a subsequent trip, in a dangerously overconfident mood, I would nearly end up in enemy lines by taking a wrong turn on a footpath before being warned away by villagers.

"There will be soldiers with us all the time," the bishop assured us.

Neroun, the Nuba aid worker, took the convoy's lead. Before spiriting away on his motorbike, the bishop could not resist an opportunity to tease: "Why did they give a gentle man like you such a terrible name?" Neroun, after the Emperor Nero.

A line of Nuba porters, women mostly — supplies, tin drums, boxes, sacks, suitcases, cases of bottled water, camera equipment, tripods all gracefully balanced on their heads — bounded off at an unholy pace in the blazing heat. They would arrive at our wilderness compound hours before we did.

Their compensation, the result of detailed negotiations with catechists and soldiers that would take up much of the night: a bar of soap and a handful of salt.

One of the camera bags had arrived from Nairobi with a large tear in it, Peter, the cameraman informed me, despairing that equipment had gone off into the bush without him. "If we lose batteries, we're sunk."

"Too late now," I said.

That evening, at the compound, the anxious technician found his bag, contents accounted for, and then some. The Nuba porter who had carried it had skillfully stitched up the tear.

Earlier, during the hurried unloading of the plane, a bag of salt had split, causing a minor panic among the porters. Hands methodically swept up the salt that had scattered on the ramp into neat little piles.

The sack was quickly repaired, the salt replaced — or, at least, most of it was. I could not help noticing that one of the bishop's catechists — on the scene, I was told, to guard against pilfering — slipped a handful of spilled salt into his own pocket while nobody was looking.

The promised Nuba soldiers, their rifles and grenade launchers drawn, assumed a leisurely stride alongside the march of hot, dazed, and increasingly ill-tempered foreigners, the latter preoccupied with small-talk on the merits of walking shoes, what and when we were going to eat, and the inability to get straight answers from our guide —

"Neroun, just how far are we from wherever it is we're going?"

"Not far."

Members of local Nuba defense forces rather than uniformed SPLA troops, the militiamen were armed with an array of vintage weapons, smuggled in through Ethiopia, Congo, Libya, or any of a dozen arms conduits supplying Africa's wars, not to mention the weapons they'd captured in garrison raids, the surest source of arms in this "frontline" zone.

Yusuf, one of my "regular" guards, later asked me whether I was ever afraid to be in the Nuba Mountains. (Translation: Did I feel protected?)

"Yusuf," I said, "I always feel safe with you. The only thing I worry about," pointing to the second-hand rocket-propelled grenade launcher at his side, "is that you'll ever have a reason to fire that thing!"

Just before leaving the airstrip, I had noticed a lone Nuba militia woman out of the corner of an eye, lean, wiry, underfed, carrying an AK-47 on her bone-thin shoulder. Without looking up, she grabbed a handful of salt from a porter and darted into the bush.

Neroun later told me about a legendary Nuba woman SPLA commander who, in a garrison raid, had sacrificed her life for her troops. There are songs about her, he said.

*   *   *

In a land without roads, without cars or trucks, the Nuba are brilliant walkers, agile, with an athlete's speed and stamina, a stoic's poise, heads held high, the eyes in easy but constant motion over the hills, always reading, reconnoitering the earth.

An impression only heightened by their near-total absence of talk. The only human sounds to be heard, in fact, were the team's occasional attempts at conversation.

William Saunders, a Washington, D.C., civil rights attorney and a theology buff, walking at my side, tried to get me into a discussion of whether Nestorius, the fifth-century patriarch of Constantinople, was or was not a heretic.

Saunders, a Catholic convert, with ties to politically active evangelicals in D.C., would go on to write several important monographs on religious persecution in Sudan and, along with Sharon Payt, play a role in placing Sudan, and the plight of the Nuba in particular, on U.S. foreign policy dockets.

Gradually, however, I found myself wanting to avoid conversation. Mindful of the dangers, I began paying closer attention to where I was walking, to my surroundings, to the nature of the landscape, and what, if anything, it might reveal.

An acquaintance, Dave Wicinas, a California naturalist, once wrote a whimsically serious study of urban Southern California in which he advocated hiking around town with a naturalist's vision, imagining the original terrain that the city has all but erased from view.

Here, I felt the process in reverse — an urban imagination shocked into irrelevance by the immediacy and unpredictability of nature — old senses reviving, feeling rushing back to parts of oneself numbed by modernity's cult of the daydream — the mental disengagement that permits us always, and in every circumstance, to be thinking about something else.

As I was to note later in my diary, "If the Middle East is a topography that calls beyond itself — in the fertile land's dependence on rainfall, the desert's 'intimations of immortality' — Africa, by contrast, draws us into her incarnate contradictions, not away from them. Nothing here is solved; everything is mortal. The mystery is within the earth, not beyond it. One either flees this terrible beauty for the safety of abstractions, or one decides to risk it."

It does not take anyone long to conclude that the Nuba Mountains, with or without war, is a dangerous place.

Less a single mountain range than a archipelago of low hills, the

Nuba settlement with baobab tree

Boys at the Khor (dry wash), Nuba Mountains, Good Friday 1999

Nuba Mountains, in the words of Siegfried Nadel, an anthropologist who did extensive fieldwork here in the late 1930s, is marked by "rocky chains, often little more than stony excrescences," alternating with "squat massifs," none over four thousand feet high, and "isolated hills rising abruptly from the plain."[20]

These are traversed by sandy dry washes, *khor,* in the local Arabic, which become veritable rivers in the rainy season, and broad valleys, with savannahs to the north and clay-heavy lowlands to the south.

Far from being arid, the Nuba Mountains boasts some of the best agricultural land in the country. As Nadel explains:

> The hill country itself is well watered; springs, wells and waterholes are found both within the mountain ranges and at the foot of the hills. It also has a much richer vegetation and is more densely wooded than the surrounding plains.[21]

Deforestation, though, is an issue, as Nadel pointed out more than sixty years ago, as a result of centuries of cultivation, particularly on hillsides. That historic ecological problem — one has only to think of the parched mountains of Greece and the Holy Land, once heavily forested — has been exacerbated by the war. The influx of refugees into settled areas, has led, in some cases, to indiscriminate clearing of trees for farming.

Still, the area boasts abundant, and often old-growth stands of giant nime trees, sycamores, acacia, and the dom palm, so beloved by the Nubians of northern Sudan, haraz trees with their yellow seed pods, on hilltops and in the saddles of low mountains, the grotesque, incomparably gnarled baobab and, in the broad valleys, groves of ancient mangoes.

One would have once found the tracks of many animals here, too: gazelles, giraffe, lion; but decades of mass famine and war have nearly exhausted the region's once plentiful wildlife, though dark Nuba boar still scuttle through the underbrush.

The cobbled, baroque hillsides, however, are what first seize the eye.

George Rodger, writing in the 1940s, describes the "jebel country" as "mountains curiously constructed of piled boulders."[22]

These giant-bouldered knolls, exposed to some of the highest temperatures on earth, appear like something fire-blasted in a kiln, orotund sculptures of pumice and brick. Later, when we had arrived at our compound, I sat on a rocky slope, the color of black ash, to take in the view, at first concluding, wrongly, that the place in which I was sitting must have been recently scorched by fire.

The sculptural qualities reminded me immediately of the knobbed Alabama Hills of California's Owens Valley, like the Nuba Mountains, remnant of an ancient mountain range. Like them, too, one suspects that, buried beneath millennia of silt borne by the torrents of the rainy season, the roots of the ancient range plunge deep into the earth; the weirdly beautiful massifs rising above the grass, the peaks of a hidden Sierra.

In the distance, as we walked, we could make out Nuba *tukuls* on hilltops, clusters of thatched dwellings under shade trees, or wedged in among boulders — not villages, really; more like family settlements, grouped loosely, as we were to learn, around clearings where weekly open-air markets are held.

There is much tribal variety, as it turns out, in the way family compounds are organized; but they all include numerous *tukuls*, or huts, each having different functions — cooking areas, storerooms, sleeping quarters, huddled more or less together and enclosed by high reed fences.

From a distance, you could hardly tell that they were there.

Rodger, in his Nuba writings, stresses how Nuba architecture blends with and mirrors the terrain:

They [Nuba settlements] hung so high and were so much a part of the terrain that it seemed the little pot-bellied huts, with their thatched roofs, had been taken by the handful and hurled against the mountainside to settle in the crevices, between the rocks, where the wind and the weather and the passage of time had merged them into one with the jebels themselves. Some had lodged in sheer-sided ravines, others clung precariously to the bare rock and some were perched jauntily on the tops of bald boulders like the fanciful creations of some whimsical milliner.[23]

But, one thought, it was not only Nature that had taught the Nuba to build this way; history had as well. Barely visible from the footpaths, Nuba settlements featured a lean, efficient architecture of concealment for a region that had always necessitated quick escapes.

While not much is known for certain about early Nuba history, the very diversity of languages and tribes indicates that this central Sudanese region has, for centuries, been a haven for refugee tribes fleeing persecution in the North, and the depredations of the Arab slave trade. For much of the nineteen century, Turko-Egyptian rulers, beginning with Mohamed Ali, centered their army-led slave raids on the Nuba Mountains, along with the Dinka-dominated South.

Moorehead writes of this period that, "Turkish governor-generals came up from Cairo, and although they were the worst of colonizers and explorers, they extended their grip on the Sudan with a predatory intensity."

> They educated nobody except as a convenience, . . . they explored merely to destroy, and their government was directed towards one single end: to mulct the country of all the money, cattle and human beings they could lay their hands on . . . And every governor-general was judged by the success of his slave raids.[24]

During the twentieth century, British rulers of Sudan tried more than once to pacify the proud, elusive Nuba, in some cases by torching and bombing their villages, thereby forcing them to resettle in large-scale, and well-policed, farm communities in the valleys. To no avail; the Nuba who were not able to hide simply returned as soon as it was practicable to the freedom of the mountains.

Today, Khartoum's militias and Antonov bombers have taken the place of predatory slavers and misguided colonial administrators, but the Nuba's cunning, their light-on-their-feet, decentralized ways continue to aid in the survival of the thousands who still defend themselves in these hills — a point made all the clearer by the ferocity of the government's efforts to displace them.

As a native Californian and lover of semi-arid climes, it also did not take me long to suspect that the Nuba Mountains are rich in heat-loving wildlife — snakes, for instance. (I had once tried to read an ency-clopedic account of the flora and fauna of central Sudan only to find that it gave me nightmares.) Neroun, our Nairobi-based guide, was happy to confirm my worst fears as we waded through grasslands, prime habitat for reptiles, noting the five kinds of cobra that grace the area, along with generous populations of green and black mambas. "I don't know why the snakes have to be so *big* up here," he added, as if to lodge a complaint.

Later, at our compound, when Neroun was conducting tours of our *tukuls*, the conical mud and thatch huts which would function as sleeping quarters, I noticed three hand-wittled implements leaning against the opening. One was a brushwood broom for sweeping the *tukul's* beaten earth floor, a smaller version, Neroun informed me, for ushering spiders back into the bush, and then, the stout forked stick, whose purpose needed no explanation.

Even the flora of the Nuba Mountains can be a little sinister. Talh bushes, for example, abundant everywhere in the mountains, especially along the footpaths, boast long thin thorns, which, when even lightly brushed against, are capable of gashing legs and arms and shredding clothing like razors, if one is not careful.

The Nuba, who are nothing if not resourceful, have found an apt use for the talh thorn, as "organic" barbed wire for livestock enclosures and to keep wild animals from disturbing graves.

And then there's the so-called "poison tree," stunted hillside out-growths with their wild bursts of hot-pink flowers that enliven the high desert landscape at this time of year, at the beginning of the dry season.

"They are beautiful," Neroun observed, "but don't pick them, what-ever you do. The sap's loaded with strychnine."

Days later, a member of our team who'd not heard the warning, would, with the best intentions, decorate the bishop's chapel for the holidays with splays of pink flowers spied outside the compound.

A Nuba catechist, coming on the scene, washed the well-meaning decorator's hands with the thoroughness of a manicurist, and then, with-

Water carrier, Gidel, Nuba Mountains

out a word of reproach, dug deep holes outside the compound in which to bury the blossoms — to keep them from the reach of children, he said.

One thing we learned en route to our still mysterious destination: the Nuba, used to trekking great distances, do not take breaks — especially with the approach of nightfall when the threat of militia raids grows. It took some negotiation to win concessions even for the briefest stop in the shade.

The Nuba, always respectful, paused with their guests, disarranging the burdens they carried, stealing quizzical looks in our direction as we gulped water and fanned sweat at the side of the road.

At one stop, we watched village women haul water in gourd buckets from a well to fill their large clay water jars. Some sported yellow plastic versions, watering jugs from the other world that, no doubt, made them, in addition to their light weight, highly prized.

Nearby, children played in the dry wash where several small camels native to the region were being watered or viewed the scene from the vantage point of the long branches that curved over the water hole. Again, these locals did not mob the caravan. They waved when greeted and looked on, curious, but without breaking the quiet rhythms of their own routines.

(At another stop, in a fallow field, several Nuba girls from a nearby settlement did approach us with a shy offering: a handful or two of dusty homegrown peanuts, a delicacy, we learned. Also, often their only food until nightfall.)

From what we could see, the well water was brackish. The lack of potable drinking water remains one of the central problems of the region. While the Nuba had access to good wells before the war, particularly those dug in the low lands, mass displacement has forced them to depend on shallow wells jerry-rigged in the mountains or, like this one, near dry washes, where muddy water lay just beneath the soil, and with it, the water-borne diseases that are the region's bane.

In addition, the distances between these isolated wells and the settlements they serve expose water-carriers to the dangers of abduction. Thousands of Nuba women have been carried off in militia raids on watering holes, most ending up in Khartoum's so-called "peace camps" where systematic physical and sexual abuse is common.

*   *   *

Nuba women, often the war's first victims, are no less certainly the face of Nuba survival.

While in most traditional Arabic societies, women command the shadows of the public world, here in the Nuba Mountains, women are ubiquitous presences: gathering firewood, bearing clouds of laundry in baskets, and moving water from local wells to family compounds like a living aqueduct.

"My day starts very early," Hosna Adam Khalil, an SPLA-sponsored women's association leader, told me in a 1999 interview. "I go and fetch the water. This is the most important thing. When I come back, it's time to pound the grain [sorghum]. Then the next thing to do is to collect the firewood. And then fix breakfast for the family. And then, it begins again. We have to fetch more water from the well and collect more firewood for the preparation of supper. This is the normal day."

Q. Do you have other work besides this?

A. Of course. There's farming, which I do together with my husband. We work together clearing the fields, preparing the ground, cultivating the crops. But water and firewood is a must, whether there is farm work to do or not.

Q. How has the war affected these routines?

A. Women and children are most affected by the war. You have to go long distances for water, you are not in your own place, there are no grinding mills for sorghum, there are no midwives. The woman is afraid for herself and her family. There is so much uncertainty. She is not stable in her life.

Part of the reason for the marked visibility of women in these rural districts is the grim fact that many Nuba men have either been killed or driven away by violence. No one captures this aspect of the Nuba tragedy better than the late Arthur Howe in his 1999 documentary *Nuba Conversations*, in which he films a displaced group of older Nuba women, driven from their farms by the war, who, with husbands dead and children taken to government "peace camps," live scattered across the mountains in caves and abandoned *tukuls* foraging for food, surviving as best they can, on the edge of surrender to one enemy or another.

Of their nearly depopulated area, Howe says in a voice-over:

> Here there are only women left, who are gradually being pushed out of their lands. . . . I started to realize that this mass displacement and the persistent destruction of the Nuba family by separating the men, the women and the children was not the product of this conflict, but, possibly, the main aim of this conflict.

Beyond the challenges of the war itself, many Nuba women I talked to in non-government-held areas of the Nuba Mountains expressed deep fears about so-called "Arab" cultural influences and the effect they perceived such influences having on their freedom, if not on their physical well being.

"One of the biggest things a Nuba woman is afraid of is [female] circumcision," Hosna Khalil told me during a 1999 visit.

> It's not our culture. We don't practice it here. I don't really even know all that it entails, except that women say that if you go to the [government] peace camps, they circumcise you there, the soldiers, in order to rape you or so that you can be [forcibly] married to an Arab, to get a new breed of Nuba, a next generation that is Arabized, and will do what the government wants.

"As Nuba," she went on to say,

> women have freedom. We women dance at festivals or with our age group, we have the freedom to wear what we like, to decorate ourselves, we can own our own farms — this is our culture. In Arabic culture, the men and women are separated. For a Nuba, this is very strange. Men and women are meant to be together. I wish to walk beside my husband, to be at his side. Why should I wish to walk behind him? No, this is no culture fit for a Nuba.

But the other reason for the visibility of Nuba women is much deeper: namely, the central role women play in Nuba life.

In historical terms, that's clear from the number of matrilineal tribes among the Nuba, in which tribal membership, and even, though not always, inheritance rights, are passed down through the mother's line.

Even in patrilineal Nuba tribes, women play a profound, and often leading role in culture. In ancestral Nuba religion, for example, women, at least in some tribes, can become *kujurs,* or tribal priests, some of whom function as mediators between the people and their ancestral spirits, and others of whom are thought to have particular influence over forces of nature such as rain or crops.

In addition to the possibility of religious influence, the tribal law of certain Nuba tribes requires that women be represented on administrative councils or, in at least one case — the Sha'mun clan — that women function as political representatives of the tribe.

Older women, in particular, enjoy great authority in most communities, a fact most dramatically demonstrated in the Nuba notion that esteemed wrestlers and old women of high reputation occupy the highest rungs on the social scale and are treated to the most elaborate funerary celebrations.

Nuba "singers" or *hakamah,* who have a repertory of songs celebrating ancestors and historical episodes, along with songs of love, mourning, and celebration, are almost exclusively women. Their songs can also include topical commentary on local personalities and politics, and are, in effect, a traditional channel of news and opinion in the Nuba Mountains. Romantic intrigues, the misdeeds of local or national politicians — nothing escapes the attention of these local poets.

Arthur Howe's camera captures a young woman, in dire straits, grinding a bit of sorghum, who issues a fierce warning to her persecutors on the back of a deceptively casual melody:

Do not come to this mountain
because it is forbidden.
Do not come because
the rebels have got an RPG.
Do not come
because the rebels will show you no mercy.

41

The political role of the *hakamah* can hardly be overestimated. In 2004, Darfur academics conducted peace workshops for "singers" in ethnically Arab villages in the province as a tool in decreasing the violence there, acknowledging, in effect, the immense political influence the women singers of the region wield. I was told that in SPLA areas of the Nuba Mountains that celebration songs sung at Nuba festivals have such public significance that the authorities insist on vetting the texts.

During a later visit to the region I was present at a festival during which the singer praised the valor of Nuba commander Mohamed Juma, who was present. The honoree, clearly delighted, promptly rose, bowed to the poet and, accompanied by other soldiers, pressed money into the folds of a head covering she wore.

Beyond the political dimension, Nuba women are the metaphysical enactors of what might be called the Nuba worldview, particularly as this is expressed through the medium of folktales. For one thing, the principal, if not exclusive actors in many Nuba folktales are women, and in several of the ones I heard, women functioned as saviors. There's the striking tale that forms the epigraph to this book, in which the Nuba come into existence once they accept the admonition of a heavenly figure (not unlike the Virgin Mary) to avoid violence.

But in another vivid, even unsettling tale I heard among the Tira Akhdar in 1998, a Nuba woman saves her people against Arab attack by hurling the blood of childbirth on the assailants, thus turning them into red standing stones. Clearly a folkloric explanation of the ancient red-painted megaliths still found on the top of Mount Kumu, the tale also features a Nuba woman acting as a valiant and cunning savior of the Nuba way of life.

*   *   *

Though the physical terrain is perilous, the most serious challenges the Nuba Mountains pose are to the soul.

My own resistance to Sudan had surfaced early. As soon as I landed in Nairobi, in fact. Awake on my hotel bed, on the eve of departure for Sudan, dizzy with jet lag, I berated myself for taking on the assignment, a late and potentially fatal burst of idealism, I told myself, in a fifty-plus-year-old writer who knew better than to trifle with war.

Was it fear that was keeping me awake? (Was it the mefloquine? A malaria prophylactic more powerful than tetracycline, the drug has a reputation for producing wild, even violent dreams.)

Whatever the pharmacological component in my state of mind, what I was experiencing was, I realized, something deeper than fear. It was dread. Dread, a recoiling, not merely from the dangers of war, but from mysterious, unknown dangers, the things you're not equipped to handle, let alone the interior demolitions that being alive to situations like this require.

After my last trip to Bosnia in 1997, two years after the Dayton peace accords, I had told journalist friends to count me out of the foreign correspondent business for the time being. After Palestinian *intifadas* and Bosnia, I told people, I hope no one minds if I sit out the next revolution.

Here, not a year later, I had let myself be talked into going to war again. And I wasn't ready.

During the Bosnian war, I once interviewed a Franciscan priest coordinating relief work in Siroki Brijeg, a Croatian town in Bosnia-Herzegovina. I had just pushed through a crowd of women at his headquarters seeking information about missing husbands and sons. They were holding up photographs, hoping passing journalists might know something about their fate. Ascertaining where many of their loved ones had last been seen, I was reasonably certain, as a result of information I had, that many, if not most of them had been killed. I said nothing.

Alone with the priest, I asked him, a cranky, hard-as-nails Franciscan who'd been tortured more than once during the Tito years, how a war correspondent avoids being destroyed by what he sees.

He was having none of it, of course.

"What nonsense," he said. "What has all this got to do with *you?* Your job is simple: to be faithful to the dead who have no one to speak for them. And while you're at it, try as hard as you can to be alive. You will help no one, you will understand nothing if you are not alive."

War had taught me that life and death were not opposites, still less, enemies, but twins. One is never so alive as when one allows oneself, if

43

only for a moment, to believe in death. *Memento mori,* the practice of the remembrance of mortality, today one of the least fashionable strains of Counter-Reformation spirituality, at its best, celebrated this linkage: "making the thought of death bear fruit," as the Theatine Lorenzo Scupoli wrote in 1589, in a life radically conscious of impermanence, that, as a result, is all the more deeply alive.[25]

Fortunately, at that moment, another part of the brain, determined to get some rest, weighed in with the observation that if there's this much resistance going on, then the trip to the Nuba Mountains must be even more important than you think.

That sensible piece of advice earned me a little sleep, during which there were vivid dreams of children's eyes from the Bosnian war — the gray eyes of two dead Muslim boys from East Mostar I had once been ushered in to see, killed by snipers while playing soccer — and an almost physical sense that people far away were waiting.

*   *   *

I had brought only one book with me to Africa, a compact edition of the works of poet Rainer Maria Rilke, something that would easily fit into a knapsack. In the humanitarian context, a minor act of subversion, I admit, a small assertion of the personal. Why Rilke? The choice was more a result of intuition than careful thought: Rilke seemed right for Africa, big enough somehow — the Rilke whose voice, as Robert Hass notes in his essay "Looking for Rilke," "bores into us," "arguing us back" to the poverty of great longings; the Rilke who loved the immense open spaces of Russia and its multi-domed churches because they suggested the size of the inner life; and, most especially, the Rilke of the Duino Elegies, who knew that "beauty is nothing but the beginning of terror."[26]

The night before we left, I had read a passage from one of the poet's letters to his many "countesses," the titled women who were the recipients of his deepest confidences:

"... Whoever does not, sometime or other, give his full consent," Rilke wrote, "his full and *joyous* consent, to the dreadfulness of life, can never take possession of the unutterable abundance and power

44

of our existence; can only walk on its edge, and one day, when the judgment is given, will have been neither alive nor dead.[27]

Take possession of the unutterable abundance and power of our existence.

Now, on a rise, as we walked deeper and deeper into the hills, a burst of cool wind blew across my face and down into the grassland, parting whole swaths of light-washed reeds in its wake, like the passage of an invisible being. In that instant, and much to my own surprise, the last weight of resistance, along with the depression that had lingered for days, like a low-grade fever, broke.

All I knew was that I no longer wanted to be anywhere else but where I was, in the Nuba Mountains, alive to its beauties and dangers, and that, in having made that choice, it was as if I had rubbed the sleep out of my eyes.

Three and a half hours after leaving the airstrip, as night fell, we arrived at our destination, the diocesan compound just beyond the SPLA military outpost at Gidel.

A rail-thin Nuba soldier saluted us as we passed through the garrison.

"Al-Sudan al-hadith," he said in Arabic, pointing to a weathered SPLA flag — a blue-starred triangle set on black, green, and red stripes, flying from a hand-whittled flagpole.

"Welcome to the new Sudan."

CHAPTER 2

On the Nuba and Modernity

Africa . . . is the inescapable center: Equidistant between the South and North poles, lying flat across the equator, with the earth's warmest climate, hospitable to the emergence of life in countless forms — three quarters of its surface lies within the tropics. Africa looms large in the middle of the vision field, connected to Eurasia through the Middle East. . . . Africa is the mother continent to which we all ultimately belong, from where human beings acquired their deepest genetic traits. 'We are all Africans under the skin,' says anthropologist Christopher Stringer. Africa is nature writ large.

Robert Kaplan[1]

The "Rilke" chair, Gidel, Nuba Mountains

An entry from my journal:

> Westerners inevitably come to places like the Nuba Mountains with the hope that we can be relieved, if not healed of our history, a history, we have long suspected, that, for all its wonders, has failed.

Ian Buruma, commenting on this phenomenon in a review of Donald Richie's book, *The Inland Sea,* writes that the expatriate critic Richie's travelogue through a vanishing rural Japan in the 1960s is a "quest for Arcadia," for

> half-imagined places of natural innocence where people are yet unsullied by urban sophistication and Western corruption, where "people live better than anywhere else because they live according to their own natures."[2]

The redemptive power of cultural "innocence" has, in fact, been the keynote of western responses to the Nuba people in the modern era — this, despite the suspect romanticism lurking in such hopes.

Much British colonial policy in central and southern Sudan was influenced, at least in part, by notions of unchanging tribal cultures that needed shielding from the "taint of progress."

Critics of what was called the "Indirect Rule" approach — that is, colonial administration through tribal leadership, a popular experiment in the 1920s and '30s, were quick to point out that

> the government . . . embarked on a course resolutely undeterred by the realities of the social structure. This was described by Currie, the former director of education, after a visit to the Sudan, as a "spectacle" in which administrators searched enthusiastically for "lost tribes" and "vanished chiefs."[3]

This despite the fact that, as Nadel points out, Nuba culture, even in relatively modern times, was anything but static or immutable.

It often seems as if historical traditions had been cut short by the overpowering experience of the Mahdist regime (1881-1898), which must have severed all links with a more distant — and possibly less disturbed — past.[4]

In fact, Nuba tribes, at least since the late nineteenth century, have been remarkably mobile within the confines of their region, shifting their settlements, as conditions change, from hilltop to slope. Tribes have detached themselves from mother-tribes in search of better land, absorbed influences from other neighboring cultures, and come to vary widely in their traditional understandings of their origins.

In a far more serious vein, photographer George Rodger (1908-1995) went on the soul-searching African journey that brought him to the Nuba Mountains in the wake of his coverage of World War II for *Life* magazine, but, more to the point, as a response to his harrowing firsthand experience of the liberation of European concentration camps in April 1945.

He was the first photographer to enter Bergen-Belsen. He told the BBC in 1989,

> I was with four Tommies in a Jeep, and amongst the first to get in and the horror of it affected me tremendously. I was talking to a very cultured gentleman and he was absolutely emaciated and in the middle of the conversation he fell down dead. . . . The dead were lying around, 4,000 of them and I found I was getting bodies into photographic compositions. And I said my God, what has happened to me? . . . It had to be photographed because people had to know and so I just couldn't leave it. . . . But at the same time I swore I would never take another war picture and I didn't. That was the end.[5]

Rodger kept that vow, and after recording the German surrender in May, he started planning his return to Africa.

"I just had to get rid of the filth of war, the screams of the wounded,

Nuba tukul

the groans of the dying," Rodger wrote. "I sought some spot in the world that was clean and untrammeled — tribal Africa."[6]

That search for "old Africa" led Rodger, through many disappointments, to southern Kordofan and the Nuba in February-March 1949, where, in fact, he did find something that he was looking for. Here, the photographer's writings on the subject are at least as revealing as his famous images.

At the heart of Rodger's admiration for the Nuba — manly prowess in wrestling and bracelet fighting aside — is his perception of the profound goodness in Nuba culture, of the Nubas' deep humanity.

Nuba wrestlers at festivals, winners and losers, despite the fury of battle, laugh together at the conclusion of their contests and join equally in the feast. Even in the savage bracelet fights of "the wildest of Nuba tribes," the Nuba of Kau-Nyaro, a severely wounded fighter will not tend to his gashes until he has "shyly" offered his gift of three eggs. To Rodger, the effect of the gesture was as powerful as the fighting that had preceded it. This perception dominates Rodger's photographs as well, as Carole Naggar writes in her essay "George Rodger: Witness to Mystery":

> Again, in the Nuba series, Rodger, standing inside the Nuba hut, shot a wonderful backlit picture of the Nuba man carrying a gourd. The light flows and softly outlines the contours of a muscular but relaxed body, hinting at the hidden dimension of the tribe's life: their extreme shyness, delicacy and concern for their visitors. In his book, "Village of the Nubas," Rodger recalls that these giant men would wake him and his wife Cecily in the morning with a muffled beat of their drums, and would bring them a breakfast gift of eggs and milk in their outstretched palms.[7]

I do not know a single writer on the Nuba who does not remark on this contrast: the harsh landscape, with its unforgiving challenges — challenges that have always necessitated making an art of suffering, cunning, and perseverance — and the deep gentleness that defines the Nuba manner, on the other.

Another entry from my journal:

The hard land that could have made them bitter, instead has made them kind.

*   *   *

Since they were first published in 1966, the Nuba photographs of Leni Riefenstahl (1902-2003) have been nothing if not controversial. Where Rodger's Nuba images are quietly deferential, the camera angle often forcing the viewer to look up to the subject, Riefenstahl revels in close-ups and the aesthetics of Nuba bodies. Critics from Susan Sontag to anthropologist James Faris have not hesitated to cry foul.[8]

Given Riefenstahl's earlier work, particularly her documentaries, *Olympia* on the 1936 Berlin Olympics and *Triumph of the Will*, based on the 1935 Nazi Party rallies in Nuremberg, that should come as no surprise.

Legend has it that Riefenstahl saw Rodger's now-iconic image of the victorious Korongo wrestler in the 1950s, and wrote to ask the photographer where she might find the tribe — and offered him a thousand dollars to introduce her to the wrestler. "Knowing your background and mine," Rodger wrote back to Riefenstahl, "I don't really think we have much to communicate."[9]

As Faris observes, it was a grotesque irony that Rodger, who had come to Sudan to flee the horrors of the Nazi Holocaust, should find his work the unwitting inspiration of Leni Riefenstahl.

Faris, an expert on the Kau-Nyaro Nuba,[10] has, since the 1980s, become something of the German photographer's nemesis, censuring her (repeatedly) for her paternalism — she had the irritating habit of referring to Nuba among whom she had worked as "*my* Nuba" — and for a photographic record of Nuba life that, he argues, is marred by arranged shots, contrived (and paid-for) spectacles, and a sensationalistic, culturally distorted focus on Nuba nudity:

She makes it clear [in her memoirs] that she was not interested in anyone in the Southern Nuba area in clothing or who went to school. (Riefenstahl actually notes with pleasure her success in undressing people for their photographs).[11]

Later, in the late 1970s, all this attention backfired against the Nuba themselves, as the newly independent government of Sudan, embarrassed by images of "primitive" Nuba in the western press, began to police remote Nuba villages, pressuring the Nuba to abandon their way of life, criminalizing nudity, and outlawing their traditional fighting contests.[12]

For example, in an interview for a 1983 BBC documentary, Kordofan's governor declared, "from an Islamic point of view, Nuba culture is very ugly and must be eradicated." He is shown distributing clothing to naked Nuba.[13]

But even Riefenstahl, for all her predictable, and wrong-headed focus on naturism and "free love" among the Nuba (her interpretations of Nuba personal mores and nuptial customs are quite fanciful), finds herself most anxious to preserve the Nuba's moral culture, especially when she finds it weakening in the face of modernity:

> Although the Nuba have had to fight hard in the past to defend themselves against slave-hunters, they are a peace-loving people. Robbery and murder are despised and rarely occur except for the traditional goat stealing. However, there is one exception. The introduction of money has had a negative influence on their character, and this was sadly apparent to me during my last visit in 1969. During my earlier visits, my crates could be left in the open, unlocked, for months, but now this was no longer possible.[14]

And she introduces her later book, *People of Kau* (1976), with an account of her unsettling return to the Mesakin Nuba of earlier expeditions:

> We soon noticed many changes. Anyone had been at liberty to walk into a Nuba house in the old days, but most of the entrances were now barred with tree trunks. Theft, which had once been unthinkable among these people, was a rarity no longer. . . . The young men who return from the towns . . . come back fraught not only with money but with pernicious and rampant diseases which were formerly unknown in their village communities. . . . The age of paradisal innocence was dead.[15]

Nuba mother and child awaiting medical checkup

What is clear in the work of both photographers, despite radical differences in attitude, is the mutual recognition that in their Nuba images they were catching last glimpses of an endangered human consciousness.

As Peter Hamilton writes of Rodger:

[He] was conscious that the fragile relationship of man with nature, which took such intriguing forms in the remoter regions of the continent, was balanced on the cusp of change. He wanted to record as much of this richly textured and 'primitive' life as possible before it slipped away for ever.[16]

55

As for Riefenstahl, one has only to recall the bitter finality, if not hubris, of the title she chose for her collection of Mesakin photographs, *The Last of the Nuba.*

*   *   *

There was never much leisure time in the Nuba Mountains where we were concerned, certainly not much time for reading or reflection that wasn't a matter of plotting out questions for interviews or catching up on note taking. What little opportunity there was for such things tended to be in the late afternoons, when the day's heat was highest, when short naps or *al fresco* showers beckoned in the hour or two before supper.

Most days at this time, I took out the Rilke volume I'd brought with me and read something. The heat and the density of the day's experiences tended to make anything ambitious out of the question — a random thumbing of pages, letting the eye fall easily on a poem or a phrase, more a species of divination than reading, testing what sort of resonance a passage might have in the middle of Africa.

As it turned out, I found myself, day after day, drawn back to the same page. Not to one of Rilke's great or signature poems, but to a single late, untitled, possibly unfinished lyric, written in Muzot, Rilke's final retreat in Switzerland, in 1925, the year before he died.

As many commentators note, the diction of these late Rilke poems reads like something from an ancient text, recalling Rilke's travels in Egypt before the First World War, when, in a 1911 letter to his wife, Clara, he marveled at

> the incomprehensible temple-world of Karnak, which I saw the very first evening, and again yesterday, under a moon just beginning to wane: saw, saw, saw — my God, you pull yourself together and with all your might you try to believe your two focused eyes — and yet it begins above them, reaches out everywhere above and beyond them (only a god can cultivate such a field of vision).[17]

But, even more, the fragment reflects the poet's last serene preoccupations in the midst of pain and disease. Rilke wrote the poem in mid-

October when, as Ralph Freedman writes in his magisterial 1996 biography of the poet,

> [S]till in pain, and feeling increasingly weaker, Rilke tried to resume his life. The first weeks [mid-to late October] were the worst, made harder to bear because the root of his suffering defied explanation: he simply felt suspended between life and death.[18]

Rilke would succumb fourteen months later to leukemia.

The poem begins, in Stephen Mitchell's translation,

> Now it is time that gods came walking out of lived-in Things . . .
> Time that they came and knocked down every wall
> inside my house. New page. Only the wind
> from such a turning could be strong enough
> to toss the air as a shovel tosses dirt:
> a fresh-turned field of breath. O gods, gods!
> who used to come so often and are still
> asleep in the Things around us, who serenely
> rise and at wells that we can only guess at
> splash icy water on your necks and faces,
> and lightly add your restedness to what seems
> already filled to bursting: our full lives.
> Once again let it be your morning, gods.
> We keep repeating. You alone are source.
> With you the world arises, and your dawn
> gleams on each crack and crevice of our failure . . ."[19]

It was the final line that caught my attention:

> ". . . and your dawn
> gleams on each crack and crevice of our failure . . ."

In Rilke's prayer — for that is what it is — the gods' dawn is to be praised for exposing the cartography of our failure: our full lives, already filled to bursting, that resist the restedness of the gods, their se-

57

rene possession of hidden sources of life, their presence in the actuality of things.

There is no facile or sentimental transcendence here; Rilke's gods and angels live, as Robert Hass observes, in an "ambience of pure loss."[20]

Nor does the poem pray for rest in some abstraction or emotional state, but, on the contrary, in the actuality of the real world — wind, dirt, field, breath, water, of "lived-in Things."

And the poet isn't the least bit sanguine about his, or our, chances to turn the new page to which the gods invite:

> ". . . Time that they came and knocked down every wall
> inside my house . . ."

No, it is not nostalgia for some Arcadian age that Rilke bids us entertain in the poem. It is the far more challenging notion that modernity, with all its ceaseless, even purposeless striving — our full lives — has silenced what poet Octavio Paz has called "the other voice," the ancient witness of "an antiquity without dates" that, in Paz's view, poetry preserves, and which, in the case of modern humanity, is heard only in defeat.

"We are living through a change of times," writes Paz,

> not a revolution, but, in the long-standing and profoundest sense of the word, a revolt — a return to the origin, to the beginning . . . We do not know whether we are experiencing the end of modernity or its renewal. . . . If, as we hope and believe, a new form of political thought is coming into being, its creators will be obliged to listen to the other voice. That voice was not heeded by the revolutionary ideologues of our century, and this explains, in part at least, the cataclysmic failure of their plans. It would be disastrous if the new political philosophy were to ignore those realities that have been hidden and buried by the men and women of the Modern Age. . . . The other voice is not the voice from beyond the grave: it is that of man fast

Nuba family

asleep in the heart of hearts of mankind. It is a thousand years old and as old as you and I, and it has not yet been born. It is our grandfather, our brother, our great-grand-child.[21]

A note from my journal:

> If you're looking for the twenty-first century, don't bother with New York or Paris. Look for it in the Nuba Mountains.

*   *   *

I was reading the poem sitting on a crate, leaning against the wall of my hut in the meager shade afforded by the overhanging thatch. Not incidentally, I was doing considerably more brushing away red ants than reading.

I noticed a Nuba neighbor watching me, probably a refugee "squatting" at the edge of compound land, the same man I had observed early that morning skinning a goat for the feast. Intrigued, Peter, the cameraman, had insisted on filming the whole episode as the Nuba, with only a dull axe, made an efficient business of the goat.

As we greeted each other, he asked if he might see the book I was reading.

"English," he said wonderingly, as his hand turned the pages, a language that, since the SPLA made it one of the official media of instruction in non-government zones, carries with it for insurgents a transgressive mystique, the mystique of freedom and engagement with the outside, non-Muslim world.

The way the man held the book, the way he calculated its weight in his hand, as if the words themselves had mass.

Books are scarce commodities around here, and not only because of the isolation. While education is coming to the Nuba Mountains, and with it, textbooks, the land itself is not an especially hospitable environment for such delicate merchandise.

Like everything else in the Nuba Mountains, the termites here are the largest, most vigorous specimens known to humankind; and, along with the earthen floors and lack of furniture, they make books seem especially unsuited to the terrain.

Hardier, less vulnerable knowledge retrieval systems seem called for, ones that can fend for themselves — memory, say.

Either that, or the inevitable "solution" one veteran missionary proposed to me one day: "Metal furniture, metal cabinets," he assured me. "It's the only way these people are going to get an education."

In my hut, I nestled the Rilke book in my porthole-sized window, along with candles and flashlights, but the toast of Prague had to be shielded from the ravages of nature, from its paper-and-glue-eating constituencies, at any rate, in a plastic sheath.

The next afternoon when I went out to read, I found that the crate had been moved. Instead, there was a handmade chair waiting for me outside my hut. It was freshly made, you could still see streaks of light green in the axe-planed wood, and the twine seat was taut. I figured that the farmer I'd spoken to the day before must be my benefactor, but when I went to his *tukul* to thank him, he, seeing my approach, walked away at a fast clip, as if he had urgent business.

CHAPTER 3

Dances for the "New Sudan"

Our first task in approaching another people, another culture, another religion, is to take off our shoes, for the place we are approaching is holy. Else we may find ourselves treading on men's dreams. More serious still, we may forget that God was here before our arrival.

M. A. C. Warren[1]

You are the reconcilers unknown to the world, your suffering the hidden gift . . . the Bethlehem into which Christ always chooses to be born.

Bishop Macram Max Gassis,
sermon to the Nuba, Christmas 1998

Nuba dancing at sunset

I woke early on Christmas morning, at first light, to the sound of distant drumming: a soft tattoo coming from a dozen directions. Five beats, pause, as if setting the tempo, then five more, pause, followed by a steady pulse the pace of a brisk walk.

The drummers' fits and starts suggested nothing so much as a crack-of-dawn rehearsal, which, as a matter of fact, it was.

For days now, the small hamlets that dot the hillsides had been abandoned for clearings in the bush where Nuba traditionally prepare their festivals (*sibr* in Arabic). Nuba Catholics from all over the Heiban area and beyond were arriving for the feast, settling themselves in tribal and family groupings in the vicinity of a large grove of sycamores locals call *Konju*, where an outdoor Mass would be celebrated later that morning.

In the dark hut, I eased myself off the handmade *angareb*, the traditional low bed of wood and twine, with the care even a day or two in the Nuba Mountains had taught me. Flashlight in hand, I checked my boots before slipping them on, as I'd been warned to do, for scorpions. No idle precaution: On a subsequent trip, a Nuba farmer hobbled to our compound in crippling pain from a scorpion sting; and the intrepid Ian Mackie, a British agronomist working in Sudan during the Second World War, devotes a whole chapter of his memoir, *Trek Into Nuba,* to the "days of throbbing discomfort" and stupor that followed a run-in with one of the local specimens.[2]

I had finally managed a get a reasonable night's sleep. This I chiefly credited to the late-night arrival of a Nuba catechist and his family who had settled themselves into the *rakuba,* the shelter abutting my sleeping quarters. After nights of disconcerting rural silence, the low rumble of good-natured small talk and the stream of jokes that kept my neighbors laughing into the small hours eased me at last into sleep.

Pulling on my clothes, I ventured outside into the blue-gray light.

There, in front of my hut, at least, one of the night's mysteries was solved: the minor scuffle I had heard outside my door toward morning. Blood and entrails were scattered over the gravel outside. Hyenas or wild dogs, apparently, had killed a goat and deposited the little that was left on my doorstep.

I wandered to the edge of the hill, looking for the source of the soft drumming that had awakened me. Though my vantage point afforded views over grassland in three directions, the gathering crowds of Nuba in the lowlands were imperceptible in the dense foliage. The drumming alone disclosed them.

*   *   *

The Nuba Mountains are situated in the geographic center of Sudan, approximately 30,000 square miles of rocky hills in the shape of a horseshoe, about the size of the state of Maine, in Sudan's south central Kordofan province. It boasts, as Nuba scholar Ahmed Abdel Rahman Saeed has noted, the most fertile land in the country, and, with that, its richest and most diverse cultural mix.[3]

As such, the Nuba Mountains have always signified more than geography. Hidden, so to speak, in a continent-sized country,[4] the region functions, in political terms, as Sudan's center of gravity, "the north of the south, the south of the north," as locals say, heartland of its soul, frontline not only of a contemporary political conflict, but of Sudan's deeper and more fundamental contradictions. Chief among these is the attempt of its northern elites to impose a single cultural and religious vision on a land of tribes. The Nuba Mountains are, thus, the natural frontier of Sudan's long and terrible war with itself.

Though they give their name to the region, hills actually constitute less than a third of the total area of the Nuba Mountains. The majority of the land rolls out in clay plains — the region's famous "cotton soil" — either shaded in low forest or farmed.[5]

Not surprisingly, the fertility of the Nuba Mountains has historically attracted the attentions of outsiders seeking grazing land, or relief from the drought that nature periodically inflicts on northern semi-arid areas of Kordofan.

Besides the myriad Nuba tribes, perhaps a fourth of the region's inhabitants are Arabs, mainly herders and traders, along with the Daju, an offshoot of a tribe hailing from the province of Darfur, and the Fellata, descendants of West African immigrants to Sudan.[6]

The very name of the province in which the Nuba Mountains are located, Kordofan, underlines the antiquity of both its human and agricultural fertility. "Kordofan," some scholars believe, is a word of Nuba origin. According to this view, *Kordu* denotes "human," and *fan* refers to "land" or "country," hence *Kordu-fan*, "the land of humans," the habitable, cultivated land — this, in contrast to the north's inhospitable deserts and the Sudd, the vast seasonal swamps to the south created by the Nile.[7]

A mirror image of the land they inhabit — not a single, unbroken range, but clusters of peaks, "island-hills"[8] intersected by valleys — the Nuba have evolved a supple regional identity as "the people of the mountain," coupled with an unusual degree of tribal diversity.

The Nubas' dual loyalties to region and tribe show up in the most basic exchanges. Ask a Nuba about his origins, and he will typically reply: *"Ana min jebel,"* "I am from the mountain." A Nuba will declare his tribal affiliation — "I am Tira," or "I am Otoro," with reluctance, and only if you insist.

That said, the traditional saying that there are as many Nuba tribes as there are hills is, as Nadel points out, only a slight exaggeration. By his criteria, there are more than fifty distinct ethnic groups in the Nuba Mountains,[9] displaying a considerable diversity in ethnic stock, culture and language.

Linguist Joseph Greenberg identified thirty-three languages among the Nuba, while, according to another study the Nuba Mountains plays host to perhaps one hundred mutually unintelligible vernaculars and some ten distinct language groupings.[10]

This appetite for diversity within a common Nuba culture extends, remarkably, to religion. Religious tolerance has been one of the hallmarks of Nuba life in the modern era, since the region was opened up to organized Muslim and Christian influences in the nineteenth century. While reliable figures will not be available until a proper census can be taken (the last systematic one was in 1955), the Nuba include sizable communities of Christians, Muslims, and followers of Nuba traditional religions.[11]

It's not uncommon to have followers of three different religions within the same family.

It is also clear that this "negotiated" inclusiveness is a point of pride for the Nuba. As SPLM civil administrator Mohamed Juma, a Nuba, put it to me:

The Nuba Mountains should be an example for the whole world. For example, I am a Muslim. As another example, [Kordofan] governor Yusuf Kuwa, Muslim. His wife is Muslim. He's got another wife who is Christian. All his children are Christian. They are happy, they're fine. There is no difference at all, no fanaticism. This generation is coming up as one of living together. This kind of hysteria that was brought our way by Hasan al-Turabi . . . they want to finish whatever is called African and they want to do it through religion, they want to use Islam for political and strategic goals. . . . But religion is for God, and the country is for all. We in the Nuba Mountains stand in their way, our way of life, our freedom stands in their way.[12]

Palm Sunday cross, Nuba Mountains, 1999

(Juma himself, by the way, is married to a Christian.)

Gerd Baumann, a leading anthropologist of the Miri Nuba, describes it this way:

> All Miri people, villagers and migrants alike, are free in their religious practice. . . . They are obliged, however, to respect their fellows' emphasis on other religious practices. Thus a villager is free to build his own mosque, . . . and to go on pilgrimage *(haj)*. . . He is not free, however, to demand of others that they follow his example, or to deprecate their reluctance. Nor is he free to opt out of the priestly rituals and natural observances that within each village maintain the order of nature.[13]

That last suggests one of the inner keys to the suppleness of Nuba culture. As Father Pasquale Boffelli, a Comboni missionary who has worked in Sudan for more than fifty years, related:

> What you have to understand is that the glue that holds the Nuba together is traditional African religion. Islam and Christianity are fine because they're seen as supplements, enrichments. This allows a great deal of flexibility and openness in Nuba society. But make no mistake about it, traditional Nuba magic, cosmology, symbolized by the *kujur* [the traditional Nuba priest], quietly undergirds everything.

"On the other hand," Boffelli went on to say,

> this 'folk Christianity' still has value; it is a conduit for Christian values, for grace; it, too, fertilizes and challenges aspects of Nuba life. Then, of course, there will always be the 'tough Christians,' the real ones, and they will shame you with their purity, their devotion.[14]

The great Nuba scholar R. C. Stevenson similarly notes that,

> the penetration of Islam into the life of the Nubas follows the usual well-known processes of infiltration and syncretism which have been described for many tribes. Cultural elements become partially

Islamized, or are remodeled and continue as before with an Islamic *cachet.*[15]

If Nuba culture "tolerates" a bewildering degree of linguistic and religious variety, it has historically been bonded by a common way of life centered on agriculture.

Unlike the Baggara Arab cattle herders that dominate northern Kordofan, and the Dinka tribesman to the south, for whom, in different ways, cattle raising is central, every Nuba man and woman is first and foremost a farmer. As Nadel notes, while the Nuba have small herds of livestock and goats, proficiency in farming has been, from time immemorial, the hallmark of Nuba life.[16] Skilled and resourceful cultivators, the Nuba clear fields in the clay plains called "far farms," their most productive agriculture, with elaborately terraced "hill" or "near farms" and smaller garden plots worked closer to home.

Traditionally, cultivation is done by hand, with the aid of simple implements, hoes or spades. The stable crops include *dura* (sorghum), bullrush millet, maize, *simsum* (sesame), groundnuts, and *lubia* (peas or beans); as well as *shatta* (peppers), cucumbers, *daraba* (okra), calabashes (gourds), and melons; also tobacco. All this is planted during a single rainy season that runs from May to September, and harvested between November and January.

Before the war, as a 2001 NRRDO report makes clear, the Nuba were surplus food producers and regional exporters of grain and cattle. Since the mid-1980s and the onset of war, Nuba farmers in rebel-held zones have been forced to live and cultivate on marginally arable land, with the result that Nuba crop production in the 1990s fell more than tenfold, most livestock were lost, and the Nuba today are barely able to grow enough food for their basic needs — difficulties compounded by the necessity to defend themselves and their improvised "war agriculture" from militia raids and aerial bombardment.

We had arrived in the Nuba Mountains in late December, toward the end of the harvest, when the last of the sorghum and other staples had been stored, and the Nuba faced the long distance run of the dry season, six months before the sowing of new crops.

War has sharpened this perennial challenge with the seasonal onset of Khartoum's military incursions, the so-called "dry season offensives," that have made these months between rains the most dangerous time of the year.

*   *   *

The situation of the Nuba on this Christmas morning was especially precarious.

Once again, inadequate rainfall over the summer months had produced poor harvests — two years in a row. On top of that, the region was still reeling from the effects of 1997's "dry season offensive." Code-named "Operation Long Jump," Khartoum's bold February-April incursion, the most devastating in five years, aimed at breaking the back of Nuba resistance once and for all. And while it failed to achieve that objective, the campaign did succeed in destroying much of the agricultural infrastructure that had enabled thousands of insurgent Nuba to persevere.

Ironically, the offensive's commander was himself a Nuba, Brigadier General Mohamed Ismail Kakum, from Talodi in the southeastern part of the Nuba Mountains. Over his many years in the Sudanese military, the General's tactical style had earned him the nickname *El Amsah,* "The Eraser." As the conduct of the campaign bore out, it was no idle metaphor.

For more than three months, regular troops, with tanks, armored vehicles, helicopter gun ships, and Antonov bombers, aided by militias and garrison units, shelled, looted, and burned village after village, killing, displacing, and abducting thousands in the most densely populated areas under SPLA control.

As many witnesses of the siege recounted, it was scorched-earth warfare at its most thorough.

But while thousands of civilians were killed, agriculture and the food supply was the principal target of the campaign. The Debi-Tabari-Regifi-Um Dulu area, focus of the siege, is one of the most fertile agricultural zones in the Nuba Mountains, capable, not only of supporting its own population, but of growing surplus crops for displaced Nuba in other areas as well.[17]

In attacking centers of large-scale Nuba agriculture, government troops and militias sought to put pressure on the fragile food resources of other rebel-held zones, thereby tightening the noose of hunger around the whole region, edging Nuba in SPLA-controlled areas closer and closer to the brink of famine.

"Tell me about famine," I had asked a youthful Ferdinand von Habsburg (yes, *those* von Habsburgs), now an adoptive African, the bishop's director of relief operations.

"Well, it's not about 'living skeletons,' if that's what you mean," he said.

By the time people get into that shape, the sort of thing you see all the time in the media when they want to show what hunger is like, it's too late. They're already past the point when you can do anything for them. . . . The problem is that few westerners have ever thought about what it means to feel hunger, because they've never experienced it themselves. So, it's fair to say that although people in Nuba are soldiering on, throughout the year, they're continually feeling hungry.

Now the gap between hunger and famine: that's when the human body deteriorates so much, over a period of months, that you simply don't have the strength to go out and look for your own food. It doesn't develop overnight, but when it happens, it happens very quickly. And the problem is, then, that help comes too late. People say, "These people don't look like they're starving, they're all right," and, suddenly, it just all falls apart. Last year we had this situation literally collapse within sixty days. Suddenly people were running away from their villages in droves, people were dying. Hunger advances step by step, but when there's a genuine food crisis, when food is suddenly unavailable, people just collapse.[18]

But, more than anything else, it's the creation of "peace camps" in government-controlled parts of the Nuba Mountains, principally near larger population centers, that suggests that the aims of Khartoum's "hunger campaign" are far more ambitious than merely "starving out" the enemy.

The idea of "peace villages" dates back to 1988, to the proposals of the government of Sadiq al-Mahdi for resettling southern Sudanese war refugees; but it was left to the radical regime of Omar al-Bashir and Islamist ideologue Hasan al-Turabi to make them a centerpiece of the regime's *jihad* against the Nuba.[19]

In 1991, the government expelled foreign aid workers from the Nuba Mountains and refused to allow the United Nations and international relief agencies to deliver food and other necessities to so-called "rebel-held" areas of southern Kordofan. Instead, Khartoum set up its own "relief" centers, *kariyet al salaam,* ("peace villages"), under the auspices of *Da'awa al-Islamiya* ("Islamic Call"), a militant Islamic relief agency, the Sudanese Red Crescent, and other charitable agencies attached to the National Islamic Front (NIF).

According to many reliable accounts, including the 1997 report of Gaspar Biro, special rapporteur on Sudan for the United Nations' Commission on Human Rights, in these "peace camps," Khartoum's agents offer food and medical assistance only to those willing to convert to Islam.[20]

"The people have no choice," Neroun Phillip, the relief worker, told me. "They're already past the point of desperation by the time they reach these camps. Perhaps they've already watched a child or two starve. They'll do anything, *anything* to save the rest of their family."

Biro's 1997 U.N. report also charges that Nuba women are routinely raped in these camps and used as soldiers' concubines, that Nuba children are sold into slavery, and that the able-bodied are frequently conscripted into Khartoum's militias, the People's Defense Forces (PDF), to fight against their own people — charges confirmed at every point by Nuba in the areas we visited.

By the early 1990s, Khartoum officials had set up nearly one hundred "peace camps" in government-controlled areas of the Nuba Mountains and, at least initially, elsewhere in northern Sudan.

As a student interviewed by African Rights in 1992 wrote of his search for relatives in camps near El Obeid:

Dead bodies are an ordinary sight in these camps and in El Obeid. Sometimes dogs will bring human parts to the house. The dogs have developed a taste for human flesh — there was one case where dogs attacked a living person who was lying under a tree. In Um Hietan even the chickens are turning savage. Death is now something normal in the Nuba Mountains.[21]

The "peace camps" represent, as de Waal asserts, nothing less than a plan for the ethnic cleansing of the Nuba Mountains, for resettling whole populations of rebel-controlled zones and areas contested between the government and the SPLA.

It was a plan for titanic social engineering and political repression on a scale never before seen in Sudan.[22]

And, as of Christmas 1998, it was succeeding.

That year the U.S. Committee for Refugees chair Millard Burr noted that the government operated seventy-two peace camps in the Nuba Mountains, with a population of 172,000, sixty percent of whom were "war-affected" Nuba. He went on to wonder, in print, whether Khartoum's declared "peace by force" plan in the Nuba Mountains, announced with great fanfare by the government at the end of 1997, was the harbinger of Khartoum's "final solution" of the Nuba question.[23]

*   *   *

Morning breezes swept over our compound as the starkly beautiful hillscapes flushed with rosy light. The air was touched with the smell of grass fires and with distant snatches of song — the "pointedly topical" grindstone songs Nuba women sing while they work,[24] refrains of Arabic *daluka* love songs, or the improvisations the Nuba make up on the spur of the moment on everything from local politics to soldiers to the story of the Three Wise Men.

Riefenstahl describes the ubiquitous role music plays in Nuba life this way:

Nuba youths with rababa (lyre)

Every Nuba boy, youth, and man, and almost every girl, owns a musical instrument they have made for themselves. . . . Most of these instruments resemble a primitive lyre, but of different sizes, shapes and types. . . . The sounding-board is made of a calabash cut in half and covered with a skin with several holes burnt in it. . . . The Nuba use five strings, preferably made of steel, which they buy from the Arabs in exchange for tobacco leaves or *dura* [sorghum]. These strings, attached to a simple round peg, can be tuned individually by loosening or tightening. Before the Nuba play their lovely tunes, they often spend a long time tuning the instrument. It is interesting to note that each Nuba composes his own melodies and creates a whole repertoire. . . . On waking in the morning the Nuba immediately reach for their instrument; . . . and in the evenings their tunes sound from the cliffs where they sit in front of their houses; they sound all around the neighborhood for the Nuba even play their inimitable melodies while walking.[25]

The bishop, I noted, was up and about — probably searching for the raw materials with which to make something that might pass for a cup of coffee. The young seminarians, Dominic and Francis, southern Sudanese, with Brother Isaac, a Nuba, were already at their chores. The young Nuba women who served our compound, Hawah and Rosa, had lit fires, and water was already heating in kettles.

Though constructed of local materials — wood, stone, clay, and thatch — ours was not entirely typical of Nuba enclosures in the area. After all, we had solar panels, though these were mounted, with touching incongruity, on hand-whittled posts, and foodstuffs from another world, the tea bags and potatoes and other luxuries we had brought with us from Nairobi, and, if my memory serves me, a bottle of decent Scotch to warm the nightly *al fresco* discussions with the bishop, long, free-wheeling sessions under the stars we dubbed the "Parliament."

In most other ways, however, our compound was organized like other Nuba family enclosures, around a central *tukul* — ours had a tree growing in the middle — with various smaller thatched huts serving as sleeping quarters, kitchens, animal pens, and storerooms. These were flanked by outbuildings: the rest-house *(rakuba)* for late-arriving guests, siestas, or private conferences, and, in a more secluded area, an open-air "shower" and the open-pit latrines, called, appropriately enough, in Arabic, *beit al-adab*, "house of the proud."

Young catechists were emerging from nearby *tukuls*, flossing their teeth energetically with green twigs torn from the underbrush.

Breakfast was on the way.

When friends ask, what do you eat up there in the Nuba Mountains, I tell them that the answer to that is in a single word: *sorghum*, a sweetish, musky-tasting grain that is the staple of the Sudanese diet, and, indeed, much of Africa's. Whatever else is available — we carry in foodstuffs in order not to deplete the local food stores — there will be sorghum. Red sorghum porridge for breakfast; for lunch, boiled sorghum; and, probably, *kisr'a*, a pancake-like sorghum bread for supper. In the Nuba Mountains, one often eats *kisr'a* with a tasty sauce made of dried okra.

The Nuba catechist whose family had slept in the *rakuba* next to my hut was also up, washing his face and hands before a bowl of water with slow, graceful movements. The catechist, Joseph Aloga Jargi, hailed from the village of Um Derdu, about a two-hour walk from Gidel, an area that had seen particularly fierce persecution of local Christians over the years.

The catechist's 1995 testimony to an African Rights team investigating human rights abuses in the Nuba Mountains, speaks for the experiences of many Nuba Catholics in these hills:

> The government began by burning churches. In August 1985 the army came and burned the church at Um Derdu. . . . A church elder, al Nur Hamoda, was taken to Heiban and killed there. Daud and Abbas were taken and slaughtered with knives.
>
> Lubi was the most dominant Christian village. The *mek* [local or tribal chief], Mohamed Rahma, was very hostile to the natives of Lubi. So the Lubi youths accused him of making many mistakes, and of making an alliance with the Arabs. The Lubi youth had an early crisis with the Arabs and began to go to the SPLA.
>
> When Mohamed Rahma saw this, he decided to rob the Lubi people by using the Arab militia. The first village to be burned was Lubi, which was burned by the army of Mendi [government garrison] in 1988. The raiders took cattle, furniture, clothes, everything. Then

the youth of Um Derdu saw what was happening and followed those of Lubi to the SPLA.[26]

As it turned out, Aloga, in addition to his duties as a Catholic lay leader, serves as the bishop's efficient radio operator, whose code names disguise the details of our flight arrangements in and out of the Nuba Mountains from the Sudanese military.

"It's not an easy life out here for my priests," Bishop Gassis noted over coffee. "Not like in Europe," he smiled with not-so-subtle disdain. "My priests work from morning to night on everything from construction projects to the training of catechists. Few comforts, no vacations, isolation, constant threat of danger."

Days earlier, at an intimate, early morning Mass for his priests and the handful of catechists who had arrived for the feast, the bishop was even more expansive:

> We have just started to celebrate the blessed Eucharist and the people are already drumming — a sign of joy, Christmas is here. Christ will be with us. We thank Him for having protected you, notwithstanding all this bombing around, aerial bombardment. We ask Him to keep you safe with your flock. This is the first thing that comes to my mind. I admire you and I respect you, and I bow my head, because I call you my heroes.[27]

Well they might be. Virtually all of the pastoral staff in this part of the Nuba Mountains — Father Solomon Ewot, the priest in charge who hails from western Equatoria; the young Father Abraham Abud, ordained only last year; Father Sylvester Kasumba, a Ugandan; along with the seminarians, volunteered for these hardship posts. Many were originally or are still members of dynamic new African religious congregations, like the East Africa-based Apostles of Jesus, founded in the mid-1960s to fulfill the dream of ur-African missionary St. Daniel Comboni that "Africa would be evangelized by Africans."[28]

The first Catholic missions to Sudan date back only 150 years, to the mid-1840s. But the history of Christianity in Sudan goes back a great deal farther than that.

Sudan has a long Christian pedigree through the Nubian kingdoms of northern Sudan, where a Nubian Christian culture, allied hierarchically with Coptic Egypt, flourished for nearly a thousand years (ca. 543-1317 C.E.). It fell to centuries of penetration by Muslim tribes and, eventually, to military defeat at the hands of the Mamluks in the fourteenth century. The last Christian Nubian stronghold held out until 1484.[29]

Catholic missions begin in the wake of Mohamed Ali's 1821 invasion of the country, which opened northern Sudan up to foreign investment. After various false starts, the Italian Catholic missionary Daniel Comboni (1831-1881) established a mission center at El Obeid near the Nuba Mountains in the country's heartland. Possessed of great energy and vision, Comboni eventually became the first bishop of El Obeid, dying there in 1881 just as the Mahdist upheaval began.

Interestingly, the Nuba played a major role in Comboni's missionary plans. As Andrew Wheeler writes,

> Comboni was greatly impressed with the promise of a mission in Nuba country.... [He] was struck with the morality and discipline of the Nuba.... The Nuba Mountains were very strategic in Comboni's thinking. He hoped to move South through the mountains, planting missions wherever he could. For him, the Nuba Mountains were the beginning of Black, non-Islamic Africa.[30]

It was not to be. The Mahdist revolution halted missionary expansion in Kordofan. And, for various historical reasons — British colonial policy and Khartoum's expulsion of foreign missionaries in 1964 among them — Catholic life could not be reestablished in the Nuba Mountains until the 1970s.[31]

Earnest, hardworking, prayerful as they seem, these priests have had to come to terms with the unique challenges of serving in a remote and difficult land, where life is hard, where help is far away, and where malaria, disease, and the perils of war are very near.

As a seminary professor in Nairobi confided to me in a later interview, the toll life in Africa's rural districts takes on priests, even the most dedicated, is high. Alcohol addiction as well as priestly concubi-

Bishop Gassis celebrates Mass in a Nuba tukul built around a tree

nage is not unknown where the nights are long and where clergy are abandoned for months or years on end to their own devices.

"Only the ones who are spiritually grounded survive," he said. "If they're just poor boys from villages who've become 'somebody' once they wear a clerical collar, they're quite capable of anything."

"I could have chosen a different life," the twenty-five-year-old Father Abraham told me one night, "but I chose this one. I want to be with these people."

When asked what he prays for, he said, simply, "that my health holds up. You can only be in a place like this if you are strong."

A Christmas Eve Mass under the stars the night before had brought representatives of the more than seventy full and part-time catechists to the compound. Many had traveled for days on foot to celebrate Christmas with the bishop.

It is a delicate moment for the Church in these parts.

With new parishes established in Gidel and Kauda, and especially with the introduction of full-time clergy, older catechists must adjust themselves to working with, and under the authority and supervision of priests, most of whom are young enough to be their sons, several barely out of seminary.

Some like the veteran catechist, and permanent deacon Musa (Moses) Arad, or other early catechists, Paolo Challo and Gibril Tutu have labored alone among the Nuba for decades at a time when the diocese could not spare priests for such isolated "parishes." Attached to the more than seventy "chapels" set up over a large area — most as simple as a grove of shade trees, catechists teach the fundamentals of Catholic faith and lead non-Eucharistic prayer services in far-flung Nuba villages.

They also mediate disputes, survey needs, solve practical problems, and share the privations of their people.

Full-time catechists earn about $100 a year, although most are compensated in more precious commodities, such as blankets, soap, and salt. Increasingly, they are the "shock" troops of the bishop's ambitious plans for emergency aid, food storage, agricultural development, and water sanitation in the Nuba Mountains — efforts, it is hoped, that will permit thousands of Nuba to avoid starvation in the coming year and build a viable, if spartan, life for themselves and their families in the midst of war.

"The Church could not have survived in this part of the world," says Bishop Macram, "without catechists." It's a point that has not been lost on the *mujahidin,* the Islamic paramilitary groups who have tortured and killed hundreds of these lay leaders in the course of the past decade.

It should be noted that among the reasons militias have singled out catechists is their political as well as spiritual influence.

By the late 1970s and early '80s, regional officials, alarmed by signs of independent political activity in the Nuba Mountains, were putting pressure on Nuba chiefs and Muslim religious leaders to suppress dissent in the rural areas. Given the government's Islamization policies, limiting the expansion of the Church was a priority. Following standard colonial procedures, Khartoum sought at first to work through local tribal authorities.

As Father Butros Trille, a Nuba priest serving in the El Obeid Diocese, and an early pioneer in Catholic activity in the Nuba Mountains, recounted to me:

> The government always keeps far away. It controls through surrogates. They bribed the local chiefs to inform on local Christians, and even to lend their aid in persecuting Christian leaders, threatening them, burning down churches, and so forth. But the effect this had was to weaken the influence of the traditional leaders on young people, who saw them as "doing the bidding of the Arabs," and incline them even more to the SPLA, which was by the 1980s trying to recruit in the area. The government always tries to instigate division; but sometimes it backfires, as it did in this case.

By the early 1980s, more direct methods were employed.

> Paolo Adlan was the first catechist to be killed; that was in 1983. The killing and torturing of catechists, along with schoolteachers really escalated the conflict in the Nuba Mountains. First of all, because it caused many of the catechists to flee to the South, initially to save their lives, but eventually to join the rebels; and then, because the catechists were influential, they helped lead the people toward rebellion and the SPLA.[32]

*   *   *

The Nuba drumming had started up again, louder this time, laced with the sound of women trilling with their tongues — the characteristic ululation that women make in times of victory or happiness throughout North Africa and the Middle East.

Not "Hark the Herald Angels," surely — something much closer to the real world of Bethlehem than that, the world of mangers and shepherds, the world of the *anawim,* the biblical poor, for whom religious faith is not a matter of private comfort but fierce, cosmic hope. As Luke's Gospel has the Virgin Mary sing in her vividly subversive *Magnificat:*

> He has scattered the proud in the imagination of their hearts,
> he has put down the mighty from their thrones,
> and exalted those of low degree,
> he has filled the hungry with good things
> and sent the rich away empty.
>
> (Luke 1:51-53)

As I looked beyond the compound toward the tree-shaded clearing some half-mile away, from which the sound of drumming came, where Christmas Mass would be celebrated later on that morning, I noticed for the first time that there were eagles circling low over the grassland. I had no idea what role the eagle might play in Nuba folklore, whether such a sight might be a good or evil omen, but I knew that, in the midst of that joyful morning, the circling eagles made me uneasy.

A hilltop village only a few miles away had been hit by a Sudanese Air Force bombing raid on the Nuba Mountains a week before, and that had only been the latest in a series of bombardments that had started last August, local people said.

Despite the festivities, people were jumpy about the growing and unpredictable threat from the skies.

II

Word of the impending attack came during Christmas Mass. Several thousand Nuba Catholics had assembled for the festivities in a grove of sycamores.

It was a distinctly "African" affair.

The "entrance rite," so to speak, included the bishop and his party jumping over a bull, which had just had its throat cut, to the trills of Nuba women.

Not an exclusively Nuba custom, "bull jumping," in one form or another, is typical of many African cultures. The Dinka have a similar ceremony. Bull jumping is also a feature of ancient civilizations, appearing, for example, on third-millennium-B.C.E. Minoan frescoes in Crete where the ceremony clearly has a sacrificial meaning. Guests for whom the festival is offered ritually implicate themselves in the killing of animals to be served later at the feast.

Each member of our party, one by one, therefore, had to be persuaded to leap, walk over or otherwise surmount the shuddering bull before joining the crowds that had assembled for Mass.

Afterward, the meat, along with that of other livestock slaughtered in the course of the day would be distributed to those attending the ceremony.

Years later, at the start of the first visit of an American church delegation to the Nuba Mountains in 2001, a queasy American prelate, who had participated in perhaps one-too-many bull jumping episodes in other parts of Sudan, muttered, on being escorted carcass-ward, "Does the church have no influence with these people? Why is such savagery still allowed?"

(Yours truly was one of his escorts. Bishop Gassis had a firm grip on the other arm.)

"Don't be silly," Gassis huffed, "this is Africa," dragging the reluctant churchman to his fate.

A youth group, trained by some of the bishop's younger catechists, greeted us with characteristic Nuba songs set to Christian texts in Arabic, to the accompaniment of drums made out of leather stretched over every conceivable size and sort of container, from milk cans to gourds.

It's part of the Nuba character: isolation has made them masters of improvisation. Everything is recycled and retooled for use: Remnants of truck tires become perfectly serviceable sandals; tins of vegetable oil become percussion instruments. The Nuba even convert the weapons used against them into useful objects: We saw anti-tank shells converted into classroom bells, and the bomb casings dropped in air raids refashioned as agricultural tools.

Children in a tree, Nuba Mountains

Children took up positions in the sycamore branches as the bishop made his way to the altar set up at the far end of a nave of trees.

Jubilation was in the air, a fact not lost on Bishop Gassis himself, who lifted his crosier rhythmically in the air before the crowd, like the older Nuba men do their staffs on days of joy. In the singing and the drumming, the Nuba, if only for a moment, had allowed themselves the luxury of forgetting about the war that has claimed more than a third of their number in a decade.

Festive attire was the order of the day. Most of the women had flowers or ribbons woven into the cornrows they had plaited in their hair. Swaths of colorful cloth purchased in prewar days from *jellaba*[33] markets in the North displayed themselves to splendid effect. Traditional musical instruments such as ceremonial horns and *rababa*, a kind of lyre, had been brought. Drums of every size and description — "crying low," as the Nuba say, in their ground bass against the somersaults of "high crying" tenor drums. Young women waved small wooden crosses made of sticks or palm fronds. Nearly a hundred were there to be baptized; twenty-five to receive Confirmation from the bishop.

Only a few yards away, young Nuba soldiers of the local defense forces stood guard in a kind of ragtag nobility, with their ancient Kalashnikovs and hunting rifles.

Back in the makeshift church, the bishop had begun the Mass in Arabic, flanked by the four priests assigned to this frontline parish and representatives of the catechists garbed in white tunics the bishop had brought with him from Nairobi.

Sitting on benches to one side of the altar were civil administration officials, and commanders of the local SPLA brigade, including the chief of staff Yusuf Karra Haroun, and the charismatic sub-commander Mohamed Juma Nayel, currently adviser to the SPLA governor for civil affairs.

(I once came upon a row of Nuba soldiers marching in step down a dusty dry wash to the "front," chanting Mohamed Juma's name.)

Like most of the SPLA officers present, Juma has been associated with the insurgency in the Nuba Mountains since the mid-1980s, and is something of a regional war hero, having been one of two intrepid commanders who, against all odds, held off the most massive government attack to date in the region, on Jebel Tullishi in 1992.[34]

During that engagement, the government mobilized more than 45,000 men, including artillery and air defense battalions, along with *mujahidin*, paramilitary forces, and, it is claimed, Iranian military advisers, against a Nuba force of three thousand SPLA soldiers. The insurgent forces, led by Commander Ismail Khamis Jellab and Alternate Commander Mohamed Juma, held off the siege for six months before government troops withdrew from the area.

*   *   *

The news came in the midst of the homily. SPLA radio operators had intercepted a coded message from military authorities in Khartoum, operating out of the air base at El Obeid, the regional capital, ordering a Christmas bombing raid on the Nuba Mountains.

By now, it was already mid-morning, the time when raids were most frequent. The plane, or planes, might already be in the air.

The thousands of Nuba assembled in the clearing for Mass were a clear target. What's more, time was of the essence: In case of attack, it would take more than a few minutes for such a large crowd to beat an orderly retreat to the relative safety of the bush. A decision had to be made at once. While the bishop was still speaking, a priest approached him, whispering the message.

In a voice brisk with urgency, the bishop told the people about the impending attack.

"The plane is coming to bomb. Everyone get under the trees." No panic, no outcry, not even a hint of surprise greeted the bishop's words.

The discipline, the serenity for which the Nuba are famous, marked every face as the people prepared for the worst. Those wearing lighter clothing were moved to the shadiest areas under the trees with the children, before whom lines of adults ranged themselves as human shields. The crowd shifted itself into its new positions without a word.

"Don't be afraid," the bishop told them. "We are all together. The Mass will continue."

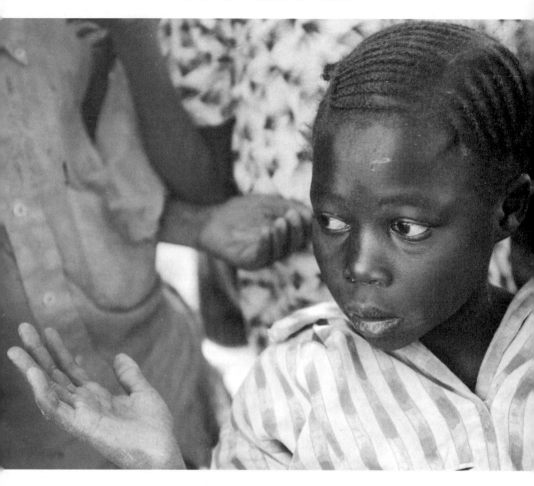

Girl praying, Nuba Mountains

*   *   *

"Ente gallabta sharq, ente gallabta mu-u-u-t . . ." "Evil you have con-
quered, O Christ, death you have vanquished . . ." — Arabic refrains
driven by the steady pulse of Nuba drummers shot out over the hills as
the nearly three-hour Mass came to an unhurried close.

Here, in the middle of Africa, one could feel the gravitational shift

88

that Church experts on missiology, mission studies, and, indeed, many cultural commentators have long noted: The shift from the hegemony of an increasingly secularized western hemisphere where faith is viewed as a cultural option, to Christianity's growth sector, its vital front line in Africa and Latin America, where faith is still a matter of life and death.

These Nuba, especially the newly baptized, are under no illusion that their public profession of Christian faith renders them anything but more vulnerable to the vicissitudes of war — their families the special targets of paramilitary violence, the "object lessons" of militia raids.

Not that Nuba *Muslim* insurgents haven't been targeted by the regime.

In fact, Alex de Waal calls it the "darkest secret of the Sudan government,"[35] the victimization of Nuba Muslims by a regime claiming to act in the name of Islam.

Dating at least from 1993, Khartoum has officially declared that Muslims in rebel-held areas are "not true Muslims," their mosques illegitimate, thereby giving its troops a license to kill "rebel" Nuba Muslims, too.

Along with priests, catechists and other religious and civil leaders, Nuba imams have perished in the government's war against the Nuba, their mosques burned to the ground, their holy books desecrated by government troops.

The *fatwa* (religious ruling) of April 1992, which provides the "legal" basis for the government's anti-Nuba *jihad,* states that

> An insurgent who was previously a Muslim is now an apostate; and a non-Muslim is a non-believer standing as a bulwark against the spread of Islam, and Islam has granted the freedom of killing both of them.[36]

But there was a political as well as a religious dimension to the Nuba's refusal to allow Khartoum's threats to break up their Christmas. The thousands of Nuba Catholics in these hills, along with their Muslim and traditionalist counterparts, pride themselves on their hard-won status as a free people.

Even in the midst of war and hardship, the Nuba, along with other anti-government forces, are working to build civilian structures that defy Sudan's long history of colonial rule, military dictatorship, and descents into what scholars of the region have aptly called the "politics of ecstasy" — the country's periodic and disastrous flirtations with messianic religious enthusiasms — a trend that goes back at least to the nineteenth century, and is amply, if cunningly, reflected in the program of Hasan al-Turabi, ideologue of the current NIF regime.

Nuba and their southern Sudanese allies have a name for the now and not-yet reality they have forged in the areas they control — *al-Sudan al-hadith*, the "new Sudan."[37]

Dr. John Garang de Mabior, chairman of the SPLM, and one of the "founders" of the insurgency, who, it's safe to say, has been nearly as controversial a figure *within* his movement as outside it, summarized the political aims of the "new Sudan" this way:

> We believe the new Sudan represents the future and the hopes and aspirations of the Sudanese people, in that the new Sudan is based on a Sudanese commonality — a social and political commonality that belongs to all of us, irrespective of race — whether we are Arab, whether we are of Arab or African origins. Nations are formed as a result of the historic *movement* of peoples, as in the U.S.... So we aspire to a new Sudanese dispensation in which all are equal, irrespective of these localisms which we inherit out of no choice of our own.[38]

Given the brittle political realities on the ground, the term suggests not so much a policy, as a state of soul.

"We may die on these mountains," said a Nuba commander to me one day, after delineating the famine prospects for 1999. "But we will die free."

"The non-government areas of the Nuba Mountains," one official in the civil administration explained, "[constitute] the only place in Sudan where there is an actively functioning democracy today."

As de Waal writes:

> Self-determination has become a political slogan and a promise in contemporary Sudan. In the mouths of political leaders it is an event (a referendum) and a decision (to separate or combine into a unitary or federal state). But in the hands of villagers in the Nuba

Mountains, it is something far more profound: it is a process whereby ordinary people are able to discuss and debate, influence their civil and military leaders, and begin to take control of their collective political destiny. What the outcome of this process will be, nobody knows.[39]

A Nuba parliament, the Advisory Council Conference, has been meeting in SPLA-controlled areas of the Nuba Mountains since 1992. And, according to reports, it's a feisty affair. Civilians outnumber soldiers in the assembly, and at a 1997 session in Kauda, civilian leaders reportedly took SPLA commanders to task for lack of discipline among troops in the region.

(After initial SPLA campaigns in the region in the late 1980s, during which soldiers committed many human rights abuses, even in villages sympathetic to the SPLA, current civilian-military problems principally involve looting. As African Rights notes, "many SPLA soldiers are dressed in rags and have virtually no possessions. The temptation to use their weapons for self-enrichment — or simply for obtaining food, is severe."[40])

Convened in the midst of catastrophic Nuba setbacks in September 1992, the Council fatefully voted to back the war effort rather than surrender to government demands, thus launching the Nuba on a unique experiment in popular wartime democracy.

"Should there be peace," writes de Waal,

the Nuba people will be the most organized, articulate and democratic in presenting their demands to the Sudan government, the SPLA, the region and the world.[41]

(Antonov bombers launched raids in the Nuba Mountains to prevent the parliament from meeting last year. Fortunately, according to eyewitnesses, the cluster bombs had been wrongly fused and failed to explode, though a school teacher who was in the process of evacuating primary school students was injured by shrapnel.)

"Ironically, despite the war," the official said as we left the Mass site, "this is a joyful place."

*   *   *

The drone of the approaching bomber pierced the layers of the day like the rise of an argument in a crowded room.

Nuba at the clearing had just settled in for an early start on the songs and drumming that would lead to dancing and wrestling matches when the heat of the day had passed.

As for the bishop and his party, we were in the middle of the half-mile hike back to the compound for lunch when we first heard the sound of the steady drone through the haze of far-off singing.

While most of the crowds had dispersed into smaller groups, the arrival of the Antonov had found us in a dry wash where the Nuba water their cattle. It was the worst possible place — fully exposed to view from the air. The cattle and their herders, now fleeing across the sandy river bottom for the safety of nearby thickets, are a frequent target of the raids.

Suddenly, everything was moving: a guardsman had seized the bishop's hand and was pulling him into the shade along the riverbank. Running alongside the bishop, I looked back to see Peter, the cameraman, white as a sheet, mapping out camera angles as he darted for shelter behind us, keeping the camera running all the while. People were now scurrying everywhere into the bush, their eyes scanning the hot, cloudless sky for a hint of the bomber's whereabouts.

Who were the pilots manning these planes, one could not help wondering. Raw recruits with little sense of the terror they unleashed from the bowels of their craft, men following orders, true believers, mercenaries, war profiteers?

Nuba radio operators told me on more than one occasion that the Antonov pilots whose communications they intercepted spoke something other than Sudanese Arabic, raising speculation about the degree of "internationalist" involvement in the NIF's dirty work.

As David Aikman, former senior correspondent for *Time* magazine, wrote in a 1999 article on "the world's most brutal, least-known war":

The Antonovs are said to be piloted at times by Libyans and mercenary pilots from the former Soviet Union. They fly around 25,000

Nuba woman, 2004

The Kauda bus, 2004

Nuba women at Mass, 2004

Nuba tukul, interior with bed

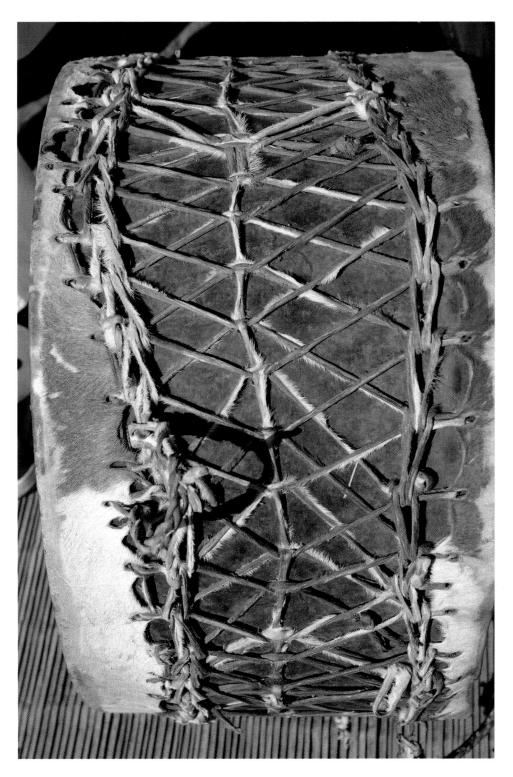

Drum, Nuba Mountains

Turkana woman, Lokichokio, Kenya

Commercial district, Lokichokio

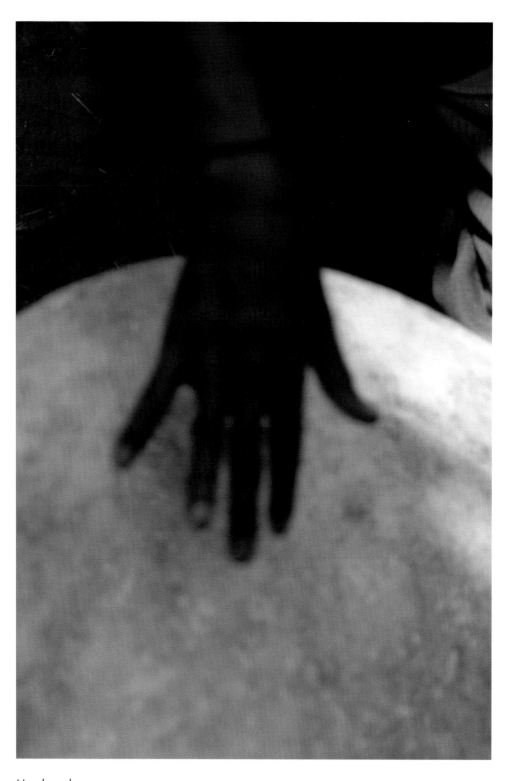

Hand on drum

Dancing feet, Turalei, northern Bahr al-Ghazal

feet and higher, out of range of normal anti-aircraft guns, wreaking havoc with complete impunity.[42]

"Where are we going, bishop?" Peter cried, panting.

"They've thrown the bombs," the bishop said, when we'd finally stopped under a tree to catch a collective breath. "They've already dropped them, the bombs," he reiterated, cocking his head in the direction of the white plumes of dust that rose over a hilltop some distance away.

"Where they have the military operations."

Back in the clearing under the trees, where the Mass had been held, Father Tom Tiscornia, an American Maryknoll priest working with the bishop, later told me of the strange silence with which the Nuba had greeted the sound of the approaching plane.

Tiscornia, who was a fairly recent arrival in the Nuba Mountains, hails from Hoboken, New Jersey, and has served in various African posts, especially in Tanzania, since 1973. His association with Bishop Gassis goes back to the late 1980s when he worked for the Diocese of El Obeid.

It was his first experience of aerial bombardment.

"It was as if they could hear it, as if they were listening for it through all the drumming," he recounted. All of a sudden, the music stopped, as if on cue. Nuba grouped together very closely in the shade, he said, without a word.

In all the anxiety of that moment, there was this strange peace, this serenity there under the trees. Over the noise, people could hear the plane, and they ran toward the trees and others out into the bush area. Under the trees, where I was, there were several hundred people: children and women and young people and old people. You could hear the drone of the plane, and the closer it got, the noise level just decreased, decreased, decreased until there was dead silence under the trees. I said to myself, 'Man, these people go through this every day of their lives, and here it is Christmas Day, and after such a great celebration, the anticipation of singing and dancing, and to have to go through *that*. But for them, it just seemed like an ordinary thing. My thought was, I was happy to be there with them. Whatever was going to happen was going to happen to all of us.[43]

The immediate danger had passed, though it was some time before we learned the exact location of the attack. Eventually, reports filtered back that eight bombs had been dropped in the area with some collateral damage to property, but because most people had left their villages for the festivities, no one had been injured that Christmas day.

The bombings would come to be a daily routine in the week that followed: the nine-a.m. alert, the drone overhead, a frantic search of the skies for the bomber's position, the sound of concussions, plumes of smoke, and, a few hours later, eyewitness damage assessments.

The air force's aim was off that week, so the raids did little more than keep the nerves on edge. Still, the regime's aerial hunters had served their purpose: To make life for the Nuba, without potable water and a reliable food supply, even more precarious, to destabilize their settlements, destroy livestock and the agriculture the Nuba had managed to coax from the stones.

*   *   *

Christmas Day. Late afternoon. The drumming had started up again. With the light mellowing across the grassland, we accompanied the bishop to a clearing just over a rise from the compound, a traditional tribal place of assembly, sheltered by an amphitheater of hills. The threat of bombing raids now past for the day, the Nuba, with gentle defiance, had begun to dance.

I arrived alongside Mohamed Juma, outfitted for the occasion in his best African caftan. Angling for a vivid reply, I asked him what he made of the juxtaposition: bombing raids and festivities.

"Understand something," he smiled. "In celebrating, we are also fighting."

I never found out what the ancient name of the hilltop was where we sat in a huge circle applauding good-natured Nuba wrestlers with their ankle bells, and the Nuba "singers," the poets who had already transformed the day's events into *jir sibr,* "celebration songs."

But "Hill of Freedom," I was told, was the new name local Nuba had given the large circular clearing where their ancestors had, for centuries, passed down the dances that memorialized the Nuba way of life.

Surely it was no accident that Nuba young people lined up there in the fading light to raise their hands in the gentle rhythms of the *Bongus*, a dance composed expressly for use in the new Sudan.

CHAPTER 4

On Lokichokio

Pay attention to me, you Lord of heaven and earth
for the love of the person you created.
The person who shoulders his spears alone,
I am in the sinful land of Sudan.
The birds in the sky are surprised
by the way I have been orphaned.
The animals of the forest
are startled by my skeleton.

Dinka Christian song[1]

Nuba boy at airstrip, Easter 1999

The first thing you notice about Lokichokio from the air are the warehouses: row upon row of World Food Program storage hangers radiating out from the town's airport like a vast industrial park. Form follows function: This is charity on an industrial scale.

Lokichokio (pronounced *Loh-kee-CHOKE-ee-oh*), or "Loki," as it is affectionately known in relief agency circles, is approached by plane from Nairobi down one of the world's major topographical features, the Great Rift Valley that runs from Tanzania to the Middle East, a low-lying outpost in a sweltering flood plain flanked by highlands.

Paradoxically, given the daunting terrain, this swath of northern Kenya can claim nearly continuous occupation by humans, and has been the locus of some of the most significant scientific discoveries about early human beings. "Turkana boy," the most complete skeleton yet found of one of humankind's near relatives, *homo erectus*, dating back more than a million years, was unearthed near Lake Turkana in 1984.

It's safe to say that few of Loki's numerous commuters would go near the place unless they had to. Only the hardiest African guidebooks mention the town, and, then, only to discourage anyone from going there.

This, despite attempts by the few carriers who service the outpost to lure travelers with cushy extras, as a flyer distributed at the Lokichokio airport cheerfully announces:

Airline X: Always working to make your travel experience to Lokichokio more comfortable. Yes, you guessed it: We're adding toilets on all our Nairobi-based flights."

Even Africa "rough guides" sensibly urge their up-for-anything clientele to hop a flight, with or without latrines, rather than risk the roads to Loki. A recent guide cites post-1996 upsurges in banditry, adding that, if you must travel to Loki by land, it's strictly by convoy, and "get where you're going before 3 pm." If not, the guide advises, be prepared to give the nice highwayman whatever he asks.

Lokichokio, Kenya, the shabby, parched outpost on the Kenya-Sudan border that functions as the logistics hub of United Nations relief operations in Sudan, has been aptly called the town that desperation built. It was, until the late 1980s, a sleepy customs post at the extreme northwest corner of Kenya, ringed on three sides by Uganda, Ethiopia, and Sudan, home to a population of less than two hundred, mostly nomadic Turkana tribespeople[2] and a few luckless Kenyan border officials, eleven miles south of the Sudan frontier.

All that changed in 1989, when the United Nations chose the spot as the launching pad for Operation Lifeline Sudan, a massive international effort to relieve war-related famine conditions in nearby southern Sudan. Today's Loki boasts a population of more than 30,000, including hundreds of aid workers attached to the World Food Program and a host of other non-government agencies, an airstrip said to be the second-busiest in East Africa, along with the world's largest Red Cross hospital for war-related injuries.

The largesse from the international community literally fills the air. According to a 1998 WFP report, relief agencies at the height of Sudan's civil war were ferrying more than 150,000 metric tons of free food, cooking oil, and other provisions per year on huge C-130 "Hercules" aircraft to drop-off points in southern Sudan, feeding more than two million Sudanese, at an annual cost of more than $100 million.

The ironies abound.

Charity has not made Lokichokio a gentler, kinder place.

The profile of the local population post-U.N. is strictly border town, and rough border town at that. In addition to indigenous people and relief workers, Loki boasts an eclectic mix of international thrill seekers, journalists, smugglers, medical personnel, spies, missionaries, arms dealers — and pilots: Tough professionals for the "official" humanitarian flights that roar into Loki's skies from dawn to dusk, *and* those willing to serve the "unofficial" traffic, the pilots of conscience (or daring) who fly without government clearance into Sudan's war zones.

In addition to the sheer physical risks, the lack of insurance coverage for these unofficial adventures significantly reduces the number of volunteers. Providing some form of pilot insurance is, in fact, one of the reasons that the costs of non-OLS relief operations are prohibitive for all but the most committed NGOs.

For example, insurance costs alone for Bishop Gassis's relief flights can run into tens of thousands of dollars — this, in addition to the costs of equipment rental and the relief supplies themselves.

Given what the pilots who fly into areas like the Nuba Mountains undertake, the costs are hardly unreasonable. The security situation requires them to fly "blind," that is, without reference to Sudanese air traffic control, through difficult terrain and violent seasonal storms.

I remember one foray into the Nuba Mountains during which the pilots, flying at low altitude for security reasons, had to steer through blinding torrential rains for most of the flight.

And there's always the threat of miscalculation. On one trip, the bishop awoke from an in-flight snooze only to realize that the pilot, less experienced than others we'd hired, had misread the map and was flying close to Malakal, a government-held regional capital, thus increasing the threat of detection and shelling as our plane made its turn north to land in the Nuba Mountains.

"I tell you that's *Malakal*," insisted Gassis. "You've got to get away from Malakal!"

"It can't be," said the pilot, consulting the map for the tenth time.

Finally, as our craft passed over the control tower of Malakal's military airport (one could almost wave), the pilot reconsidered.

"Hmm, you may be right."

On another occasion, the bishop's plane put down at the wrong bush landing strip and had to make a quick exit to avoid capture by government troops.

And as one might expect so close to a war zone, Loki is the hub of far more than relief operations; it's also the center of arms smuggling into Sudan. AK-47s, communications equipment, grenades — they're all for sale in Loki's open-air market, or, more discreetly behind the ramshackle truckers' and workers' bars that line the town's one long two-lane road, with their improbable evocations of Nairobi nightlife: "Club Webbs," "The Zebra Hotel," "Fine Touch Fashion Boutique," and my personal favorite, "Cold Comfort Restaurant — ask about accommodations."

This is Graham Greene country, a landscape of boredom, intrigue, and moral bewilderment, or, as Ruth Franklin recently described the novelist's fictional terrain, "A desolate colonial outpost with unforgiving weather, which is inhabited by mid-level civil servants, simple-hearted locals, and adulterous wives."[3]

Not surprisingly, crime is one of Loki's "attractions."

Cargo trucks are routinely assaulted, their drivers sometimes killed. Relief agency security details are now a common site as thieves raid the town's relief agency compounds, often in broad daylight. The thousands of aid workers, often in transit to and from Sudan, rarely venture out of their compounds, especially at night.

Political and ethnic tensions have been added to the mix in recent years.

In the summer of 2003, Operation Lifeline Sudan had to confine its hundreds of workers to their compounds as riots and looting broke out in the town sparked by long-simmering tensions between local Turkana tribesmen and southern Sudanese refugees based at the nearby Kakuma Refugee Camp.

Eventually, Kenyan military units had to be summoned to quell the disturbances.[4]

Reasons for Lokichokio's dysfunctions are not hard to find.

Living, literally, in the shadow of humanitarian abundance, tens of thousands of Turkana tribesmen, the region's indigenous goat and cattle herders, squat in shantytowns, looking for scarce water and even scarcer day jobs with the relief agencies.

The dramatic population increase due to the arrival of western aid workers has lowered the water table, drying up traditional Turkana wells, making local herdsmen dependant on the good will of foreigners for their most basic needs.

As Duncan Rundgren, a Kenyan-born aid worker for the sole non-government organization in the area focused on the Turkana, told a reporter for the *Houston Chronicle* in 1999, international aid groups based in the town, responsible for digging thousands of wells in Sudan, hadn't drilled a single well for the people of Lokichokio.[5]

Everywhere, at the sides of roads, behind the compounds of relief organizations, at the edges of their own world, one sees the haystack-high huts the Turkana build to shelter themselves from northern Kenya's heat and dust — dry branch shelters covered with animal skins, but now as likely to sport coverings of the canvas bags the World Food

Program uses to distribute food, or plastic scraps scavenged from the agencies.

Invisible, it would seem, to relief workers who speed around in a cloud of dust and trash on Loki's roads in pickup trucks and vans, the local Turkana survive as best they can on the international community's leavings.

In Loki's open-air market, bags of WFP relief provisions destined for Sudanese famine victims, paid for by western donors, are sold in broad daylight, smuggled back into Kenya by Sudanese refugees, who then sell them to Kenyan middlemen. These, in turn, peddle them to Turkana tribesmen, who purchase back the relief supplies that fly over their heads by the ton each day to their neighbors in southern Sudan.

For the poorest Turkana, there are even more desperate solutions. I myself have seen Turkana women foraging in garbage dumped outside the razor-wired compounds of Loki's international relief agencies, or filing plastic water jars from the water spigots at the gates of relief compounds under the hostile gaze of compound guards. News reports tell stories of Turkana digging up spoiled grain deemed unfit for Sudan's famine victims, which aid workers have buried at the ends of landing strips.[6]

A scene that was to haunt me many times in transit to and from Sudan: drinking a beer at the bright, well-lit bar at the Trackmark compound, Loki's version of gracious living, complete with palm trees, Jacuzzis and CNN, watching Turkana women collect firewood in the dry wash beyond the compound fence. A few yards separate us: distances as unbridgeable as they are wicked.

*   *   *

Operation Lifeline Sudan, the largest food relief effort of its kind in history, is a child of failure.

The great famine of 1988 had consumed the lives of more than 250,000 mostly southern Sudanese, and, given the bleak combination of war and political paralysis in Khartoum, international relief agencies had been powerless to stop it.[7]

It would prove neither the first nor the last time that the world's most powerful conduits of western aid would be compelled to stand on the sidelines while Sudanese, directly or indirectly, starved each other to death. In Sudan's nearly fifty years of on-again, off-again civil conflict, hunger, far more than guns and explosives, has been the weapon of choice.

One has only to glance at the numbers.

By the late 1990s, more than 50,000 soldiers, on all sides, had been killed since Sudan's civil war resumed in 1983; but conservative estimates put the civilian death toll in southern and central Sudan for these years at more than two million, most of these from famine, either instigated or exacerbated by Khartoum's war policies, abetted in some cases by those of the other parties to the conflict, the SPLA and its dissident rivals.[8]

Not that "starvation politics" is a modern concept. Cattle and sheep-raising nomads, pressed by drought, have been raiding agricultural settlements in this part of the world for centuries, killing or abducting farmers, burning crops to settle old scores or expand grazing land.

Beyond this, weather, the Nile, and the largely untapped reserves of arable land, not to mention failed agricultural policies, has made the unholy trinity of bad harvest, famine, and epidemic a periodic fact of life in Sudan.

Leni Riefenstahl relates in *The Last of the Nuba* that

> [H]unger can be the Nuba's greatest enemy. Since they seldom have money and have few goods for barter they can buy neither grain nor cattle in times of famine. I would ask my Nuba friends how they survived these times of need and they all gave the same answer. With a melancholy smile, they would say: Nuba die.[9]

But modern, especially revolutionary, politics in Sudan has played a leading role in coaxing periodic drought into catastrophic famine.

For example, the Mahdist revolution[10] coupled with drought created the conditions for the great famine of 1888-90.

As a standard history of the Sudan relates:

Horrifying tales were told of famished beggars snatching bread in the market-places with the last remnants of their strength, of silent villages whose people quietly starved to death behind closed doors.[11]

A similar, but more far-reaching combination of corrupt government, desertification, and civil war conspired to make Sudan's latest food crisis, in the words of humanitarian Millard Burr, a veritable "whirlwind of destruction."[12]

The southern uprising against Sudanese president Nimieri's policies in 1983 coincided with the onset of a famine "of incredible magnitude"[13] that swept across the Sahilian belt, from Darfur to the Red Sea Hills, placing more than one hundred million people at risk, particularly in Ethiopia, Chad, and Sudan. By 1984, the drought, easing in some areas, had wreaked havoc in Sudan's northern provinces, principally in western Darfur and Kordofan.

As Burr recounts:

By December 1984 some 300,000 people were on the move, and village and nomadic societies in Darfur and Kordofan slowly began to disintegrate.[14]

Given government inaction and Sudan's lack of strategic reserves, pressure mounted for international humanitarian intervention.

Throughout the mid-to-late 1980s, however, political events conspired both to spread calamity and sideline all but a few attempts to save lives.

Baggara militias, armed by the government to fight rebel forces in the South, were laying waste whole counties, thereby dislocating tens of thousands of civilians, and further disrupting agriculture and the food supply.

On top of that, the fighting on both sides was hindering, if not preventing attempts to get food relief to growing numbers of internal refugees, particularly in the face of a government in Khartoum which saw such interventions as, wittingly or unwittingly, aiding the southern insurgency.

The SPLA, for its part, had an interest in forestalling food aid that came with "government assistance," and in preventing supplies from falling into the hands of government forces in the South.

Despite the attempts of various international agencies to address regional food shortages, by 1988, hundreds of thousands of starving Sudanese, mainly from the south, were fleeing into Ethiopia.

As Burr vividly describes it:

> Even as congressional hearings were being held, tens of thousands of Dinka and Luo were making their way northward . . . seeking anything edible. . . . Thousands had died along the railway lines between Aweil and Babanusa while tens of thousands lay dead on the trails leading from Aweil to Safaha, Abyei and between Bahr al-Ghazal and Ethiopia. . . . [The trails] were littered with the dying, the dead and the skeletons.
>
> . . . By March more than a hundred Dinka a day were reaching the outskirts of Muglad and the barren encampment for the displaced, where the exhausted tried to gather their strength. They huddled together surrounded by a flock of human scavengers who stole Dinka children from their emaciated mothers.[15]

In addition, ruinous government-sponsored mechanized farming schemes and land expropriations in the Nuba Mountains uprooted tens of thousands of traditional Nuba farmers in the midst of the worst drought in a century, plunging southern Kordofan, already taxed beyond its limits by the mass influx of starving southern refugees, into its own worst nightmare.

In early 1989, growing media focus on Sudan's famine crisis along with the weakness of Sudanese president Sadiq al-Mahdi's government, and war-weariness in the North, combined to create a long-awaited opening for the relief agencies. Once the agreement of the SPLA to allow free movement of relief supplies in their areas was secured, Operation Lifeline Sudan (OLS), racing against time, launched its first airlifts to the south.

Challenges were not long in coming.

The consortium had barely begun its work when an Islamist military junta seized power in Khartoum that June, sending the network into a diplomatic dance with a new and hostile regime and, by the end of the year, with the daunting if not impossible task of delivering relief supplies to war victims through the cracks in a campaign of renewed and ever-expanding violence.

In doing so, OLS frequently found itself an unwitting tool in the hands of the combatants — a development which can come as no surprise to anyone who has watched large-scale international relief efforts unfold in the Middle East and the Balkans.

As Ian Fisher wrote, in a perceptive *New York Times* piece on international aid some years ago:

> Humanitarianism is, at its core, about war, and war casts its compromising shadow over humanitarianism's good intentions. Aid, it turns out, works much better in natural disasters . . . When politics provokes the crisis, . . . things get much murkier.[16]

In Sudan it got very murky indeed.

OLS acquiescence in Khartoum-imposed "relief embargoes" in the Nuba Mountains — a devil's bargain that "saved" operations in other parts of Sudan at the expense of isolated "frontline" populations — stands out as one of its uglier choices. By providing relief to Nuba in government-controlled zones, OLS, in effect, bolstered Khartoum's campaign to starve out insurgent Nuba.

Not surprisingly, OLS's efforts did not escape the typical pitfalls of large-scale humanitarian ventures that, in the pursuit of short-term goals, create a host of unintended consequences. Chief among these are aid dependencies, with all their social ramifications, that, long-term, are nearly as grave as the crises that occasioned them. In large swaths of southern Sudan, for example, farming has virtually ceased given the reliable delivery of foreign food.

In the end, "industrial charity" looks a good deal like what poet Wendell Berry calls "industrial medicine." The point of reference of industrialized charity threatens to become, not the health or welfare of the potential beneficiaries, but "its own technical prowess," its problem-solving capabilities.[17]

As Ferdinand von Habsburg, describing his experiences of food distribution in southern Sudan, once put it:

Jamaica Hotel, Lokichokio

Think endless lines of aid recipients that relief workers who've had bad experiences have learned to humiliate into some sort of order; people waiting desperately for food who hate you with all their hearts.

As the war dragged on into a new century, OLS found itself furthered weakened by internal dissension, by Khartoum's ceaseless maneuvers to gain control over the organization's activities, particularly at its base camp in Lokichokio, and by its feckless responses to Sudanese air force attacks on its facilities and on civilians assembled at its food distribution centers in southern Sudan.

An especially egregious, though hardly isolated example of the latter occurred as late as February 2002, when a government helicopter gunship opened fire on civilians at a World Food Program distribution center in Bieh, killing dozens, despite specific government clearances for OLS operations that day.

Khartoum later expressed its regrets over the incident, calling it a "technical fault."[18]

As Burr sadly concludes, Operation Lifeline Sudan, given the circumstances, was "bound to fail." Besides its own contradictions (and, indeed, the contradictions inherent in the humanitarian enterprise itself), it foundered, for all its resources, on the shoals of a "repressive Sudanese government," and of a conflict that had "dissolved into an interminable guerilla war with no defeats and no victories, only casualties."[19]

Or, as an old man told journalist Ian Fisher one afternoon in the Nuba Mountains:

> We are not in need of clothes or salt. . . . The main thing we need is for this war to be solved. You can bring whatever you like here. If this war continues, it will mean nothing.[20]

*　　*　　*

A final note on Loki

On my way back from the first trip to the Nuba Mountains, in the first stages of decompression, awaiting the next flight to Nairobi, I had what might well be called the essential Lokichokio exchange.

"I hear you're just back from the Nuba Mountains."

The voice came from a remarkably attractive woman, armed with a glass of white wine, and moving toward me as I stood at the Trackmark bar, still travel-gritty, and fit for only the most forgiving human company. A London-based human rights expert, later research confirmed. She was decked out, for this rough-edged outpost, in what, for me, seemed a not unwelcome but incongruously elegant black cocktail dress.

The Trackmark bar, complete with faux-safari décor, was filled with relief workers back from the bush and off-duty pilots, a solid blue-collar crowd on their way to and from showers, waiting for the buffet line to form.

Startled at first, and mindful, even now of security, I am in the midst of fudging the details when she interrupts my evasions with, "Don't romanticize the Nuba." Rolled r's and a direct object that had two extra syllables.

I think she put her hand on my arm.

"Everyone romanticizes the Nuba."

CHAPTER 5

Songs on the Death of Children

"In this weather, in this storm
I would never have let the children go out;
They carried them away
And I could not protest.
In this weather, in this wind . . ."

Friedrich Rückert, "Im diesem wetter"[1]

Q: So, given the bombing, what are you going to do now?
A: We are going to persevere. We continue [with our education].

Q: Is there anything I can do for you? Is there any way I can help?
A: You can make the bombers go away.

Author's interview with an eleven-year-old
Nuba student, March 1, 2000

Church, Kauda, March 2000

Modern wars always turn out to be wars against children.

"My" wars have taught me that, conflicts that I've covered in the Middle East, the Balkans, and, now, Sudan — wars that, in the end, always conspired to bring me face to face with their ultimate victims, and, therefore, as I only gradually came to recognize, with their inner and secret dynamic. Conflicts aim at the destruction of armies, of the defenders of women and children, in order to position themselves to inflict the one irreparable wound, the wound from which no one recovers, the injury, for all its simplicity, far more consequential than the death of cities, for in the death of children, one strikes at the very possibility of hope.

There is something of this perception lying just below the surface in Israeli premier Golda Meir's oft-quoted remark from a 1969 London press conference:

> When peace comes, we will perhaps in time be able to forgive them [the Palestinians] for killing our sons, but it will be harder for us to forgive them for having forced us to kill theirs.

According to United Nations Children's Fund figures, more than two million children perished in local and regional conflicts in the decade of the 1990s, with more than three times that number permanently disabled or seriously injured, and twenty million uprooted by war, living as refugees or as IDPs, internally displaced persons, within their own borders. At any given time, hundreds of thousands of children are forced into service as soldiers, or, as a consequence of war, into involuntary servitude or the sex trade.

But such figures do not begin to suggest the enormity of the violation.

It's always seemed strange to me that events nearly always arrange themselves so that, as a reporter, I happen upon stories having to do with the effects of war on children. Strange, because it happens consistently, stumbling upon these "small tragedies" while I think I'm covering something else, and because, single and without married siblings, children are not otherwise a part of my life.

In the Balkan conflict, while covering an American relief operation's efforts to get medical supplies to the frontline, I discovered, quite by accident, an improvised "children's camp" at Capljina in western

Dog at gravesite of Muslim child, victim of Kauda school bombing

Herzegovina, near an equally improvised encampment for refugee families that had established itself in abandoned railway cars.

We arrived at the camp in the pouring rain. Local aid workers and a few U.N. soldiers had taken charge of the several hundred war orphans living there in appalling conditions. Plans were in the works to build semi-permanent housing there for them, and perhaps a school, but in the meantime, children were dying each week of exposure and disease.

I talked to one of the U.N. soldiers, who expressed frustration with the pace of construction at the camp, but even deeper frustration with his sense of helplessness before the terrors of his charges. He was especially concerned about one four-year-old boy, Ratko, found wandering in a Bosnian wood, who, according to reports, had seen his whole family slaughtered by the babysitter. The boy had not yet spoken to anyone.

"What will become of such a child?" the soldier asked me. "What will he say when he speaks again? And will we be able to endure it when he does?"

When I last saw Ratko a year or so later, he was playing ball with the staff. He had not yet spoken.

*   *   *

Kauda Foq (Upper Kauda), Nuba Mountains, Sudan, March 2, 2000

It was the sound of the fluttering pages that first drew my attention to the exercise book at my feet. Under normal conditions, the weathered pages with a child's scribbles might have gone unnoticed altogether. But only weeks before, more than a dozen young lives were snuffed out here in a hail of shrapnel. In the tense silence that still reigns over this primary school in the war-torn Nuba Mountains of central Sudan, one hears the smallest of sounds.

A dirty notebook, without cover, wedged between bricks, its pages webbed with penciled exercises in English grammar and math — smeared here and there with dried blood. It had blown here, probably, from the schoolyard. The last dated page, February 8, 2000, had a math

problem scrawled across the top, then blotches of brown stain marking the exact moment when this Catholic bush school of 230 pupils found itself the target of a Sudanese air force bombing raid.

"Maths," the last used page of the small graph-lined notebook reads, with the date, 8/2/2000, written in Roman and Arabic numerals; beneath the date, a double row of simple arithmetic in a slightly uncertain hand:

$$10 \times 7 = 70 \quad 10 \times 8 = 80 \quad 9 \times 10 = 90 \quad 10 \times 2 = 20$$
$$5 \times 10 = 50 \quad 4 \times 10 = 40 \quad 3 \times 10 = 30 \quad 10 \times 1 = 10.$$

That's as far as the young student got that day, and not only in his studies.[2]

*   *   *

"It came without warning at nine o'clock in the morning," the young headmaster Baruch Musa told me in early March, shortly after I had arrived in the Nuba Mountains as part of a team sent by Bishop Macram Max Gassis to report on the bombing.

Shells were already raining down on the schoolyard when the headmaster, in one of the school's five classrooms, shouted to students to fall to the ground.

"Stay, don't run," the headmaster shouted to the children before dashing outside to warn the classes under the trees. He had time only to scream, "Lie flat," to youngsters fleeing in terror from the blasts before he had to hurl himself to the ground.

"The sound of those shells coming right down on top of you," he related, "terrible, unforgettable."

Shrapnel whizzed in every direction. Within seconds, the yard was a scene of carnage. Five so-called "barrel" bombs, studded with nails, had been unleashed from the belly of a low-flying Russian-made Antonov MU2, the Sudanese air force's weapon of choice in its terror war against insurgent populations.

"People were already on edge," said Headmaster Musa. A July 17

Bloody schoolbook on grave, Kauda, March 2000

Unexploded ordnance ("barrel" bomb), Kauda, March 2000

bombing raid on the area resulted in the deaths of eight Kauda young-sters tilling fields. Locals described aerial reconnaissance missions over Kauda only three days before the school bombings, perhaps, they said, identifying targets.

Medical personnel headquartered at the German Emergency Doc-tors' compound in Luere reported seeing helicopter gunships in the vi-cinity February 5, three days before the school attack.

"They dropped bombs not 15 minutes from the school the Saturday before," said Musa. "They had to see the children running into the bush for cover. They knew where to strike next."

*   *   *

Kauda's Catholic primary school, Holy Cross, looks like a typical Afri-can "bush" or rural school, with its low mud and brick buildings and thatch roofs. Founded in 1998 by Bishop Gassis, it plays a unique role in stabilizing war-weary populations in the region who have been subject to decades of neglect, war, famine, and government persecution.

The school offers a muscular education. The core curriculum, an adaptation of the Ugandan syllabus, includes geography, history, math, science, social studies, English, Arabic, Nuba languages, music, and tra-ditional handcrafts.

One of the school's more "revolutionary" aspects, given the political climate of Sudan, is the emphasis on proficiency in English, along with coeducational classes, and a distinct stress on education for girls.

Six teachers, four men and two women, were on staff at the time of the bombing, including the headmaster, who is the son of Musa Arad, a permanent deacon ordained by Gassis in 1985.[3]

Of the more than two hundred male and female students at the school — of various ages, given the relative scarcity of education in any form in the region, the majority comes from Christian families, but with a substantial Muslim enrollment.

While war conditions have slowed if not halted educational oppor-tunities for a generation in the region, the character of much prewar ed-ucation in the Nuba Mountains can be gleaned from South Kordofan governor Yusuf Kuwa's colorful account of his:

119

We were taken as children to the schools. It is very interesting to explain when I started my rebellion. It is when I was in elementary school. I think I was in grade four. There was a headmaster. Of course, he came from the North. And he was always saying, "Why should these Nuba boys be taught, they should go to work as servants in the houses," or whatever. Because truly the majority of our people used to go to the North, and most of them worked in the houses as servants and in such types of bad jobs. So he was often saying, "Why should the Nuba boys be taught?" The worst part of it I remember was that when the bell used to ring for the start of the lessons, this headmaster used to come and sit under the tree, while he was supposed to be teaching us. He used to come rarely, and most of the time he would sit under the tree, or do what he wanted, without teaching us.[4]

Needless to say, Nuba *girls* could not expect to be admitted even to this grudging education.

The importance of discrimination in education as a factor in motivating a large number of Nuba youths to join the insurgency cannot, as de Waal notes, be underestimated.

[N]ot least because a large portion of the [Nuba] recruits to the SPLA are frustrated students. An earlier generation of disappointed students had simply opted out to become migrant laborers in Khartoum or other Northern cities; the generation that was in school when the war broke out had more direct ways of channeling their anger at a system that appeared set up to deny them.[5]

*   *   *

Journalists are fond of describing long-running conflicts such as Sudan's as "low-intensity" wars. But there was nothing "low-intensity" about the terror visited upon this remote schoolyard on a clear February morning.

The Anatomy of a Bombing:

The tragedy revolves around two shade trees in a schoolyard. Under the northern-most tree, forty-two students were studying arithmetic; under the southern tree, an English class of fifty-three students was assembled.

When reports of the bombing first came to my attention, I recalled that David Tlapek, who directed the documentary we made on Sudan,[6] had filmed these outdoor classes not ten months before. I got out the "raw" footage. The headmaster, Baruch, was there; the teacher, Roda Ismail, moved among the students, wearing the same blue dress she wore that day, the day of the attack; a slow pan of the faces of these earnest youngsters sitting in neat rows trying not to look at the camera; chalk boards leaning against a tree.

The first two bombs failed to hit their target, landing in a hollow a quarter mile from the school and at its perimeter. The third bomb, however, landed in the schoolyard between the two trees, leaving a blackened crater in its wake. Shrapnel moving at speeds of up to two hundred miles an hour sliced through the air.

The students who flattened themselves on the ground, as they had been trained to do, had a chance. Those who tried to run away from the blasts did not.

Seeing where the third bomb had struck, and with terrorized children breaking into a run all around her, teacher Roda Ismail tried to force them to lie down, and shifted her students to the back side of the southern tree to shield them from the shrapnel whining across the yard.

That was when the fourth bomb fell. This one exploded not in a line with the other bomb but behind the sycamore, ten feet from the shadow side of the southern tree where Ismail shielded her students. Their position left them exposed to the full force of the impact.

The fifth bomb went harmlessly astray in the dry wash south of the schoolyard.

By 9:15 it was all over. The low-flying Antonov had flown through a saddle of hills that guards one of the region's lowlands, site of the school, dropped its deadly cargo, and made another pass across the schoolyard to assess the damage. For good measure, eyewitnesses say, it dropped ordnance on nearby hilltop villages before leaving the area.

The headmaster, who had taken cover himself, rose to find students dead or dying all around him.

He ran first to the tree that had taken a direct hit, the southern tree.

They were all dead there, except the teacher, who was still breathing, and a boy with his intestines out, who was still moving. I tried to see if there was anything I could do for him. Nothing. I pulled down his shirt [to cover his wounds]. One girl there had been decapitated. When I went over to the other tree, three were already dead. One child was still alive there, but died a few minutes later. I shouted to people to take them to the hospital [the German Emergency Doctors' (GED) clinic]. Many died on the way. Some of the wounded ran into the bush, others ran to their parents in the mountains.[7]

Families, too, up since dawn, and already in the heat of the day's work, heard the blasts ricocheting across the hills.

Salwa Khamis, a widow who had lost her husband in a 1997 militia raid, roused her four children at 5:30 that Tuesday morning, and began routine preparations for the day. Gandi, her nine-year-old son, complained of feeling sick; thinking that it might be malaria, Salwa told him that he could stay home from school, and suggested that Munira, his twin sister, remain to care for him. But Munira was determined to go to school, and set off on the nearly two-hour walk across the hills to Kauda, and to an English class under a tree where her life came to an end.[8]

Miraculously, in a region without roads and vehicles, emergency medical help arrived on foot within forty minutes of the blasts.

"When we heard the explosions, we just grabbed what equipment we could, and ran for the school," one nurse said.

There, twelve students, ranging from 9 to 16 years of age, lay dead, along with Roda Ismail, 22, their teacher. Two students who fled into the bush died later of their wounds. According to Tina Wolf of the German Emergency Doctors group that provides primary medical care to

Kauda bombing amputee, Adil Kuku, March 2000

122

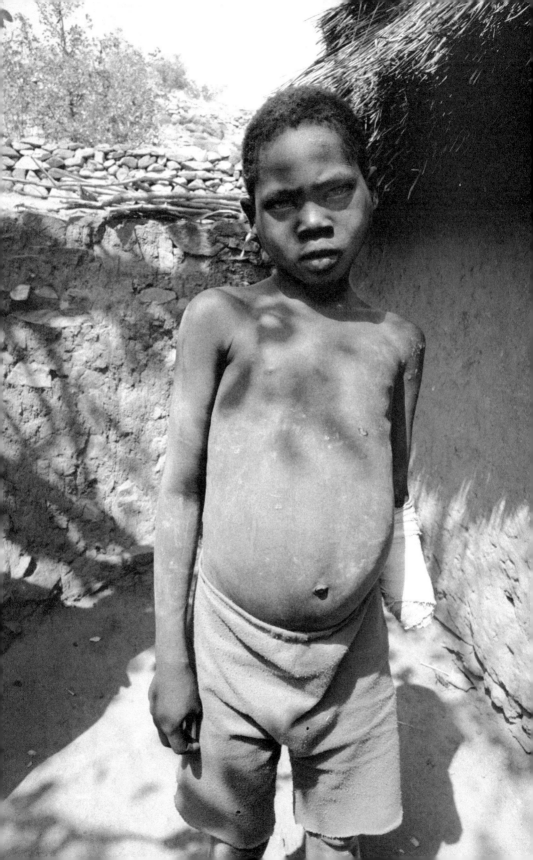

the people of Kauda, five critically wounded children perished in the days following the bombing, raising the student fatalities to nineteen.

Those who died at the scene [name, age, tribe, birthplace]:

Roda Ismail, 22, teacher, Lira, from Lira Kadro
Ruza Daliel Umely, 9, Otoro, from Kauda
Munira Khamis Bako, 12, Otoro, from Kauda
Randa Abdallah Al-Girba, 11, Otoro, from Kauda
William Abdallah Kalim, 15, Otoro, from Kauda
Maima Tutu Kudi, 14, Otoro, from Chari
Kaka Ali Shirallah, 16, Otoro, from Kauda
Tabitha Hamdan Kuku, 14, Otoro, from Kauda
Francis Peter Elamin, 11, Otoro, from Kichama
Hamid Yousif Ismail, 10, Otoro, from Kauda
Hydar Omar Kharshiel, 12, Otoro, from Kauda
Kubi Yousif Ibrahim, 13, Otoro, from Kauda
Bashir Ismail Kamsson, 12, Otoro from Kauda
Osman Rajab Arnu, 15, Otoro, from Kauda
Kuri Abdul Gadir Kuku, 11, Otoro, from Kauda.

In a dark tribute to Nuba tradition, seven of the initial fourteen dead children were Muslim, seven Christian. "Even in death," a Nuba teacher declared at the time, "the Nuba people are one."

Of the seventeen wounded, four youngsters required amputations, two of fingers, and two, more seriously, of a hand and an arm. One of the wounded had to have shrapnel surgically removed from her neck.

As I wrote some weeks later in my journal:

We came upon the small mud-brick compound camouflaged behind a low range of hills amid trees. In addition to schools and churches, medical clinics here have found themselves prime targets of Sudan's aerial hunters. Outside, in the hospital courtyard, among the hand-made cots of sick and injured Nuba and their relatives, we had our first glimpse of the survivors of the Kauda bombing. Members of the clinic's staff brought forward a boy with a bandaged wrist, Adil Kuku, age 11. When shrapnel from the blast nearly severed his hand, amputation had been the only available remedy. More tragic still, a lovely 12-year-old girl, Amani Hussien Abdallah, had lost the whole of her right arm; her left arm was also injured and her chest scarred from the blast. Even in these children, one could not fail to notice the serenity and quiet self-possession that marks the Nuba's stance toward the world. Here, in the clinic courtyard where the effects of the bombing were most evident, one sensed not terror but deep determination — *seberi*, perseverance in struggle, the Nuba call it. Nowhere more so than in the eyes of these wounded children.

And there was one further victim of the bombing.

The mother of Ruza (Rosa) Daliel was cleaning the yard around her *tukul* when she heard the sound of the approaching Antonov. A few seconds later explosions could be heard coming from the direction of the school. She ran, along with many others, to investigate.

Neighbors living close to the site saw her approach the schoolyard and tried to dissuade her from going further.

"It is too late," they told her, "there is nothing you can do." Her daughter Ruza had been decapitated in the blast. They pleaded with her not to go to the schoolyard.

"Go back home," they said. "We will bury her." But the mother could not be dissuaded. In the schoolyard, she collapsed over her daughter's broken body and died of heart failure.

*   *   *

Khartoum's apologists, used to having their way unobserved in remote locales like the Nuba Mountains, were clearly caught off-guard when the Kauda bombing attracted the attention of the international media. After all, dozens of school children have been killed in area bombing raids since 1997 without occasioning a single line of newsprint.

In this case, Lokichokio's mix of rumor and pilots proved fortuitous. The bishop's diocesan personnel, out of the field for their annual staff meeting in Nairobi, were in transit there, waiting for flights when first reports drifted in.

Maryknoll missionary Father Tom Tiscornia recorded it this way in a report:

> I had been in Lokichokio since February 4 waiting for an NRRDO plane to the mountains: It was leaving every day — *yaani BUKRA* [Arabic, "tomorrow"]. While there, in the evening, we received word of the bombing of the school in Kauda [that morning]. How awful — and it seemed that the days of the Antonov dropping [bombs] were over; they were, for a while. Fortunately, two days later the plane left and brought us directly to the new airstrip at Kauda. It was the inaugural flight!!! . . . We landed fine (I did see the mountains directly in front of us as the pilots were searching for the airstrip — anyway, God was surely with us). On board the plane were reporters from BBC, Reuters, and AP. . . . The reporters were only able to interview people who were at the airstrip since the plane was not going to wait for them to make the one hour walk to Kauda. . . . One of Kizito's people[9] had been at Kauda during the bombing and he had taken photos as well as video so at least there was a possibility of them getting some footage for news coverage. I thought that it was really good to have these people there and to be able to report to the world. . . .[10]

More than anything else, it was the video footage that galvanized world attention, however briefly, on this forgotten part of the world, and helped make the "Kauda bombing" one of the defining moments in Sudan's war against the Nuba, if not the civil war itself, spurring international and regional leaders to renewed attempts to stop the violence.

By chance, catechist Stephen Amin, 22, a second-year communications studies student at Daystar University in Nairobi, was in the vicinity of the school conducting interviews with his battered camcorder. When the attack occurred, he ran toward the schoolyard and the carnage, and was on hand to record the aftermath.

Mercifully, a broken microphone renders the footage silent.

"It was a harrowing experience," Amin told the BBC. "Children were screaming, throwing dust on their heads and beating their chests in grief and disbelief. Those who managed to say a word could not manage more than 'All are dead.'"[11]

By February 14, less than a week after the attack, the BBC had reported, "Sudanese atrocity caught on film."

As for Khartoum, the official rationales for the attack seemed to shift by the hour: The bombing was a rebel fabrication; the children were killed in an SPLA military camp; the children were guerrilla fighters; the school was next to a military garrison, which was the real target; schools are a legitimate target in a contested area; and, finally, after the video had aired, the bombing was a regrettable mistake.

As a February 16 *Agence France Presse* report summarized, "On Monday (February 14), Khartoum said civilians in the central Nuba Mountains may have been unintentionally hit in recent air strikes and said it would try to avoid such accidents in the future."[12]

(Since then, however, Khartoum's bombers have been more than usually active. A few days after the Kauda bombing, on the day after the U.S. government issued a condemnation of such attacks, air force Antonovs targeted civilian concentrations in Panryang, south of the Nuba Mountains. And on March 3, the government bombed a hospital compound in Lui, near the southern Sudanese city of Juba, killing three and injuring scores of patients and staff. The Lui bombing occurred while President Clinton's new Sudan envoy, former Florida congressman Harry Johnston, sent to pursue "dialogue" with the regime, was meeting with Sudanese officials in Khartoum.)

All the evidence on the ground points to the fact that the attack on Holy Cross Catholic School was anything but a mistake. The raids and reconnaissance activities preceding the school bombing clearly point in the direction of a deliberate attack, as do the initial declarations of Sudanese officials themselves.

On being shown the video of the Kauda bombing, Dirdiery Ahmed, a minister in the Sudanese embassy in Nairobi, Kenya, told Reuters, in a now-famous remark:

The bombs landed where they were supposed to land. The bombs landed in a military camp. The SPLA has pulled people into this military camp.[13]

The bombs landed where they were supposed to land.

127

As many journalists later noted who visited the site, the only structure near the school is a clearly identifiable church. The nearest SPLA military outpost is a more than two-hour walk away. Upper Kauda is, in fact, a new settlement, built, as its name suggests, on higher ground in the late 1990s when historic Kauda (*Kauda Tehet,* Lower Kauda), at the mouth of a wide valley, became too insecure.

What prompted Khartoum to carry out the Kauda attack, coming, as it did, in the midst of one of the regime's "charm offensives" in the West — along with a campaign to seek foreign investors for its potentially lucrative oil industry, and, paradoxically, just days after its representatives had held peace talks with the SPLA in Nairobi?

One of the short-term reasons for the attack, some suggest, may have been to avenge the killing of Sudanese Brigadier General Mohamed Kakum. Kakum, a Nuba, and one of the architects of Khartoum's scorched-earth policies in rebel-held zones in the Nuba Mountains, drove over a landmine on Feb. 7, the day before the bombing.[14]

Journalist Charles Ormondi wondered aloud in an African News Service report filed in the aftermath of the bombing whether the attack could also have been "a message to the local Catholic Bishop Macram Max Gassis that Khartoum was not moved by the awareness campaign on the tribulations of the Nuba that he was creating the world over."[15]

Directly after the school bombing, the Antonovs conducted bombing raids over another of the bishop's parishes, Gidel. The planes dropped eight barrel-bombs in the area, according to parish personnel. Locals speculated at the time that the planes were looking for the bishop's other Catholic primary school, Sts. Peter and Paul, but failed to spot it. This, probably, because the SPLA has a new anti-artillery installation in Gidel; hence, the Antonovs cannot risk low-altitude precision raids there, but must content themselves with "random" attacks.

If the intent of the Kauda bombing was to weaken Nuba resolve to remain on their ancestral land, or to frighten them into submission to the regime's campaign of cultural and religious assimilation, it has, at least in the short run, had the opposite effect.

If anything, the bombing would appear to have deepened the resistance of these Nuba. And that new determination is nowhere more evident than in the target of these attacks, Kauda's children.

"It was the children who put us all back together," Musa told me.

On the day after the bombing, the headmaster was astonished to hear that schoolchildren were waiting in the schoolyard for classes to begin.

"I went out to reason with them," he said. "Listen," he told several hundred of his charges, "Go home. I can't tell you when, or even if we'll be able to resume classes. We're all destroyed by what happened. I'll let you know what we decide."

A ten-year-old boy came up to him, the headmaster recounted.

"*Ustaz,* professor," the boy said. "Let us continue. If it is God's will, we won't die."

When I visited Kauda three weeks later school was already back in session.

II

It needs to be pointed out that Nuba children are hardly the only Sudanese children who have found themselves the objects of Khartoum's war aims. In fact, numbers alone indicate that the children of southern Sudan constitute the primary juvenile targets of the war.

By the mid-1980s, successive Khartoum governments employed slave raids as a major weapon in attempts to weaken the southern insurgency — and slave raids in this context mean, by definition, the capture of women and children.

As historian Jok Madut Jok describes it:

The first reports of slavery that appeared in the media were championed by South Sudanese journalist and politician Bona Malwal . . . during Sadiq al-Mahdi's reign as prime minister of Sudan. When allegations of slavery became widespread in 1987, Bona Malwal and Macram Max Gassis, the bishop of the diocese of el-Obeid, at the request of some members of the U.S. Congress, went to testify in Washington. . . . The question of slavery heightened the North-South

divide. Instead of investigating it, many educated Northerners concluded that the allegations of slavery were meant to tarnish the image
of the North, especially its Islamic character, . . . a suggestion that
outraged the South even more.[16]

A few courageous northern Sudanese intellectuals did report on the resurgence of one of Sudan's most pernicious cultural habits.

As Bona Malwal relates in a July 2003 interview:

> Two academics from the University of Khartoum, . . . Dr. Ushari
> Mahmoud and Suleiman Baldo set out to prove [me] wrong. . . . They
> did not believe that slavery existed in Sudan in this day and age. . . .
> But being honest academics, they stumbled on an even greater evi-
> dence of the enslavement of South Sudanese by Arab militia when
> they arrived in Western Sudan.

Mahmoud published the first major slavery exposé from a northern
perspective. He was repeatedly jailed for his efforts.

But with the advent of the NIF regime in 1989, and its determination to win the war with the South at all costs, slavery became a truly
mass phenomenon.

Malwal continues:

> It is perhaps important to bear in mind that the government in 1983,
> and indeed the current one, which overthrew it by a military coup, had
> no cultural inhibition towards slavery. Being Muslims and Arabs, it
> seemed culturally acceptable and religiously legitimate to these gov-
> ernments to enslave those who are at war against them. This is why the
> present government of Sudan proclaimed at the very start of its mili-
> tary campaign when it first seized power . . . that it was engaged in an
> Islamic holy war in South Sudan. In an Islamic holy war, slavery is an
> apparently legitimate war policy, if not wholly legal.[17]

Northern Bahr al-Ghazal was among the hardest hit areas. The region
sits on the border between Dinka and Baggara land, just south of
Darfur, on a tributary of the White Nile that local Arabs call Bahr al-

Arab and which the Dinka, the main indigenous population, call the River Kir. Abweil, Abyei, and Twic counties, one of Abyei's acting commissioners explained to me in 1998, "are the front line of the slave trade, the first places they go looking for slaves."[18]

Slavery is nothing new for the Dinka. For centuries, northern nomadic tribesmen, chiefly the Missiriya of southern Kordofan and the Rizayqat of Darfur, have raided Dinka villages for slaves. William Finnegan, in a long 1998 *New Yorker* piece on Sudan, in which he portrays slavery as the central issue of the war, quotes an old Rizayqat song that urges tribesmen to

> carry the jim gun whose fire chars the liver and the heart,
> for I need an errand boy from the black slaves.[19]

Even today, the normal colloquial Arabic word for African blacks in northern Sudan is *abeed,* "slaves." (Efforts by Sudan's propagandists in the West to explain the term away as an allusion to the submission all Muslims owe to God is, to say the least, disingenuous.)

As Jok notes,

> Long after Sudan joined the world community in ratifying antislavery conventions and formulated legal provisions that prohibited slavery, the practice persisted, . . . as its ideology has been coded into the Baggara Arabic language, folklore, daily humor and poetry. It is this long history of an ideology of dominance that Arab governments in Khartoum have always used to treat the South as a mere source of material resources, and its inhabitants as cheap laborers who are useful only when stripped of their freedom.[20]

British attempts to eradicate the slave trade during their sixty-year administration of the Sudan were not entirely successful, although central and southern Sudan were closed to northern Arabs, in part, to stamp out illegal trafficking in slaves. As we have noted elsewhere, even after the country's independence in 1956, the slave trade, let alone the racial and ethnic prejudices that informed it, were never entirely absent from the scene.

What was new in the wartime revival of the slave trade was Khartoum's policy of providing arms, direction, and military cover to Baggara tribesmen to abduct Dinka women and children on a scale unseen in more than a century. And according to local officials I spoke with in the late 1990s, it was not only the Baggara who were involved: People's Defense Forces (PDF), the so-called "Islamic" militias, and even regular Sudanese army units were also implicated in the trade. If *murahileen,* or "raiders," once descended on villages on camelback, they now arrived in jeeps and armored vehicles, with military backup, armed with automatic weapons.

The full impact of Sudan's return to the slave trade doesn't hit you until you talk to the children. In Turalei, a small settlement of Twic Dinka that the war has transformed into a haven for refugees and IDPs at the edge of swampland, children who have experienced slavery firsthand are easy to find.

Many of these children have lost whole families, some during the raids in which they were seized. Some escaped from their captors; some were purchased back by relatives after long searches, sometimes lasting months or even years, for their whereabouts; a few were rescued by international abolitionist groups such as Christian Solidarity International (CSI), based in Zurich, that attempt to "ransom" women and children from the principal northern slave centers. The going rate for adolescents and young adults in Sudan is $100, half that amount for children.[21]

The methods of capture are varied: raiding villages, scouting for children herding cattle or goats or fishing on river banks, luring children in towns with money or sweets, or, simply, making the capture of slaves a routine adjunct to military campaigns.

Branding is not uncommon. Eleven-year-old Dol Angok, captured in 1996, showed me the numeral "7" burned into the skin of his right arm.

"I tried to escape," the boy told me in a 1999 interview,

> but they [his masters] reached me on the way. They made a mark so that if I went somewhere else [i.e., tried to escape], everyone would know to whom this boy belonged. They tied my hands and I walked on foot. When they camped for the night, they beat me a lot.

Dol Angok and other "redeemed" children, Turalei,
northern Bahr al-Ghazal, 1999

Bol Kir, eight years old when I spoke to him, seized on the banks of the
River Kir with his younger sister, had an "11" carved on his right cheek.
He was captured in 1996, when he was five. He also complained of being
beaten when he failed to account for the goats his masters had sent him
to herd.

As one would expect, sexual abuse is common, and young boys and
some girls, especially those considered marriageable among the latter,

Bol Kir, "redeemed" slave, Turalei, northern Bahr al-Ghazal, 1999

are circumcised — this despite the fact that the custom, widely prac-
ticed in some Islamic contexts, is abhorrent in much of the African
world.

Showcased in discreet "slave houses," principally in Kordofan and
Darfur, the slaves are marketed internally, within Sudan, for everything
from farm labor and the care of livestock to domestic work. According
to local officials, some are exported to Libya, Morocco, Tunisia, and, it
is claimed, to Persian Gulf states.

In most cases, the children were given Arabic names and taught to
pray as Muslims.

"We are your new family," ten-year-old Teresa Arou was told by the
masters that bought her from her nomadic captors. (Her father had

134

been killed trying to save her from the raiders.) "You have lost your people, you have no choice," they said. "Either you accept living with us or we'll kill you." Her new family also insisted that she adopt the Arabic name Zaara.

Unable to stop crying, Teresa cried out to God, she told me. Later that night, she had a dream in which she saw a cross.

"A voice came from the cross: 'Why are you crying? Aren't you called Teresa? You are still who you are.'"[22]

After that, she said, her determination to resist captivity hardened. Luckily, relatives eventually located her, and after repeated attempts to buy her back, Teresa's owners were persuaded to release her.

Finnegan's *New Yorker* piece quotes Sudanese slavery researcher Mahmoud:

> Army officers, when they return from the south, often bring black children back with them. They hand them out to relatives for work around the house. People don't see this as slavery. But that's what it is.

Mahmoud calls northern Sudanese attitudes toward slavery, even among political liberals, "total denial."[23]

The size of the phenomenon, even the scale of the war resurgence, has always been difficult to ascertain. What can be said for certain is that it involves tens of thousands of women and children.[24]

*   *   *

In late 2004, I traveled to Turalei in northern Bahr al-Ghazal, after the permanent cease-fire had been signed, principally to ask questions about the dimensions of the tragedy in one of the hardest-hit counties in the south, and to find out how the reintegration of abductees was faring as Sudan's second civil war wound down.

"We still do not have accurate figures for the number of women and children taken in slave raids since 1983; but the minimum number is between 20,000-25,000 from Twic County alone," County commissioner (official title: SPLM county secretary) James Aciei said when I interviewed him in late December.

Given the momentum for peace, an official process is now underway to locate and register Dinka and Nuer women and children held in bondage in the North and to arrange for their release and reunion with their families in the South.

I asked the commissioner how many abductees had been brought back in the past year (that is, in 2004) to Twic County. An excerpt from our interview:

A. Last April, 205 abductees were put under county authority. Their photos were sent to us and we summoned the community to see if their families are here. Another 506 currently in Muglad have been "collected" and are on their way here.

Q. Can you describe the problems the returnees are going to face?

A. The immediate problem is that there is little food in the county and supplies are scarce. We simply don't know how we'll care for them. The drought is very bad now, and has been since 2000.

Q. What cultural adjustment problems do they encounter when they return home?

A. There are success stories, particularly for those who were taken as teenagers, when they had already formed an identity as Dinka. But for some returnees, those taken as very small children, for example, there is the *loss* of culture, they have been Arabized, they don't speak Dinka or Nuer. Returnees sometimes feel outsiders in Dinka society; sometimes, when they're brought back, they won't sit with Dinka. There's a whole loss of social identity. And, in some cases, there's nothing for them here — their families are gone, their village destroyed, there's no way for them to live. These often run away.

Q. Run away?

A. Women raised in an [Arab] environment where they are not supposed to see a man. When they're introduced to Dinka society where the sexes commingle freely, sometimes they run.

Q. Are there any solutions on the horizon?

A. The first thing is to get these kids to go to school, or adult education, for the adults. They then can gradually readopt the culture of their birth. The Church is doing a lot to help us with this reunion process. But we're at the beginning of a long and difficult road — Dinka society and the returnees. After the war, our cultures are scattered like broken eggs. How are we going to pick up the pieces?

III

The sun was high by the time we trudged up to the ridges of the hills that ring the fertile Kauda Valley. Visitors to these highlands, with their stone terraced settlements, learn quickly that even the simplest of errands require half-day treks over rugged terrain.

Kauda is real hill country. The Heiban *jebels*, which range as high as 4,500 feet above sea level, form the spine of this "far-flung hill range," as Nadel describes it, "composed of eight main hill chains . . . and the large plateau" of Chungur.[25] Kauda today is the central gathering place of the Otoro, perhaps the largest tribe in the eastern *jebels*, and fast becoming the center of SPLA activity in this part of the Nuba Mountains, in part because of the airstrip located at the southern end of Kauda Tehet, supply line to the outside world.

The early morning hike occasioned little if any of the banter that ordinarily accompanied such excursions. Today we constituted a party of mourners paying our respects to the families of the victims of last month's Sudanese air force bombing raid on a Catholic school in the Nuba Mountains that left nineteen children dead, along with an adult teacher.

Father Tom Tiscornia and the other personnel had preceded us along this route, paying their respects to families scattered among the villages in the days following the attack.

Locals told me that while it was customary among Nuba for villagers in the area to pay condolence visits for up to forty days following burial, such visits, given war conditions and the "instability" of the region, had been limited this time to two or three days.

Our team, consisting of Dr. David Coffey, of Montgomery, Alabama, representing the Bethlehem, Pennsylvania-based Catholic Medical Foundation, myself, and photographer James Nicholls had been dispatched to the area by Bishop Gassis, traveling in the United States at the time of the attack, to conduct a fact-finding mission on the February 8 tragedy, and ascertain what, if anything, we could do for the injured. We were also there to deliver a personal letter from the bishop to his people.

*   *   *

The veteran human rights campaigner had been in the States that month, preparing for premieres of a documentary on his work, *The Hidden Gift: War & Faith in Sudan,* and an important meeting with U.S. Secretary of State Madeleine Albright, along with a ceremony at which he would be given the prestigious William Wilberforce Award for his efforts to end religious persecution in Sudan[26], an honor arranged for him by his Washington, D.C. colleague, civil rights attorney William Saunders.

On his arrival at Los Angeles International Airport, I led him to a waiting room chair and handed him a wire service report that had just come to my attention.

> KAOUDA, Sudan, Feb. 10. Sudanese air force planes bombed a school in the village of Upper Kaouda in the contested Nuba Mountains today. Unconfirmed reports indicate that 13 [sic] students under the age of 14 have been killed.

He had not seen the report.

"It's Holy Cross," the bishop said in a quiet voice.

A few hours later, diocesan sources in Nairobi confirmed the worst:

> From Roberto [Bronzino], Nairobi, Feb. 10:
> The date Feb. 8 Kauda Foq
> 14 children dead
> 15 wounded (badly)
> no teachers (don't know yet)
> SPLA investigating
> Priests want to go back/Fr. Tom, Edward leave today

(maybe today)
Church really target[27]

That night, at the premiere of *The Hidden Gift* at Los Angeles's Museum of Tolerance, I along with others who had heard the news could hardly watch the film. The documentary had become, in the light of events, far more than a media vehicle in an "awareness" campaign. It had become a memorial to people being lost to us even as we struggled to mount a campaign on their behalf.

Gassis denounced the attack in a fierce Feb. 11 press release:

> When you think of Sudan, remember the children of Kauda. Do not say merely that the regime of Khartoum violates the human rights of Christians and ethnic African peoples. Say, rather, that it kills children. This is the true face of this war.[28]

Within days, other voices had joined the chorus of official condemnation.

President Bill Clinton issued a statement Feb. 14:

> I am deeply concerned by reports that the Government of Sudan bombed a school in the Nuba Mountain region February 8, killing and wounding many young children. It is an outrage that such egregious abuses against innocent Sudanese citizens have become commonplace in the ongoing civil war in Sudan, which has claimed over two million lives.
>
> The United States calls on the Government of Sudan to cease all aerial bombardment and to refrain from any attacks on civilian targets. We also call for full and immediate access for humanitarian organizations seeking to provide relief to war-ravaged civilians in Sudan.[29]

The president's call was echoed by the State Department, which, following the bishop's meeting with Albright, condemned the bombing.

"Calling these attacks a mistake," State Department spokesman James Rubin told a March 8 news briefing in unusually blunt language, "is simply not sufficient and not credible. These bombings must stop."[30]

But the victims of the attack required something more than high-level diplomacy. Daily briefings from Nairobi only added names to the list of the dead. Survivors might have to be airlifted out to hospitals in Kenya. That itself would take time: medical assessments would have to be made, travel arrangements expedited.

"We're losing them," the bishop said. "The children's lives are slipping through our fingers!"

*   *   *

By the time we arrived, three weeks to the day after the attack, most of the bishop's pastoral staff had returned to the field. Tiscornia, who had arrived first, not forty-eight hours after the bombing, writes this about the first days:

> When we approached the compound of the school last Thursday, it was eerie. There was a sense of sacredness about the place. . . . There were still pieces of the shrapnel strewn around from the bombs. Believe me, it was a sad moment. No one was around, but I could just imagine how it must have been two days before. . . . The mood of the people two days after the tragedy to me seemed stoic. . . . People were going around visiting the homes of the families, some almost in a state of disbelief, yet resigned that this is part of life here. . . . So I spent the following days just going around and visiting and praying with the families of those killed and wounded. . . . On Saturday I went to Kachama (Karga) for Mass at the grave of the first son of the catechist Butros. The boy's name was Francis. A simple grave covered with thorns and a cross at each end . . . [Later] we all blessed the grave with water from a calabash. Again, being there with the family, neighbors, Christians, other youth who had grown up with the boy — believe me, it was powerful, and I was grateful to have been there with them. Afterwards, we all enjoyed a meal together.
>
> 2/11/00: Friday. At 6am this morning, the Antonov flew over the area here and then throughout the day three other times. Early in the morning I see mothers going into the mountains with their children

in fear of the Antonov. . . . On the way home from the hospital [to visit the injured], at one point two women and a child were in front of me [on the path]. When they heard the plane coming, we all went down into a crevice that had been formed by the rain. What an awful way to live . . . ! Afternoon at 3:30 the Christians here gathered for Mass. . . . The children who had been there on Tuesday remembering their classmates and teacher. Some people got up and spoke. Afterwards all ate a nice meal together up on the hillside. I ate with Simon and the other catechists. The people all came to greet Simon and console him — a [Muslim] sheikh came in and prayed also.[31]

* * *

Our first stop that morning had been to the grave of Roda Ismail, the schoolteacher who had perished trying to shield her students from the attack.

Not from the Kauda area, she had been buried within hours of the bombing in a hollow near the school — a simple mound of earth covered with thorn bushes to protect it from wild dogs. She was due to be married in six weeks, at Easter.

However hastily arranged, the grave still had all the essential marks of Nuba burial, especially, I could not help noticing, the pots with their small fractures. Leni Riefenstahl describes it this way:

Large clay pots are placed on the mound and calabashes are hung . . . Piercing the clay pots means that the 'mortal frame' of the implements has been destroyed in the same way as that of the deceased through death.[32]

I knew Ismail's fiancé from previous visits, a gentle young man, Simon Kafi, one of the catechists. Father Tom had warned me that he "was truly distraught, like in a daze."

Nevertheless, Simon manfully led us to the grave where, surrounded by fellow catechists who were keeping a close, if discreet eye on him, we all knelt in silence.

The other victims of the attack were buried, as is the custom among the Nuba, near their families, in courtyards of their stone and thatch dwellings, or in secluded spots known only to relatives. One grave, along the edges of a footpath, was capped by a child's bloodied exercise book. Wiry dogs guarded others, twin mounds, for two brothers killed in the attack. The boys' uncle told us that relatives had not yet been able to lure the dogs away from the site.

"*Il barraka fikum,*" "blessing be upon you", we said in the traditional Arabic greeting of condolence to Nuba farmer Omar Kharshiel, the first of many grieving parents we would meet that day. Like many in this wind-swept valley, Omar had heard the bombing echo through the hills. Soon, relatives appeared, bearing the lifeless body of his youngest son, Hydar, 11, up the slopes.

The mother had been summoned to greet us. If the father, a Muslim, appeared to be bearing the boy's death with steely resignation, his mother, relatives told us, still spent hours alone looking out over the valleys.

Omar's family is typical of the area. Like many of the residents of Kauda Foq, he is a refugee from another part of the Nuba Mountains, eking out a meager living for himself and his family as a tenant farmer on a small plot at the edges of someone else's land. Given the fact that the perennial dry season offensives each year displace more and more Nuba farmers in rebel-held areas, such arrangements are common.

The Kharshiels are poor, even by Nuba standards: a makeshift *tukul*, few utensils, and no livestock to speak of. Like other families, this one was drawn to Kauda, in part, because of the primary school, and the chance of an education for Omar's children.

"My son was the best in English," Omar said. Others told how Hydar would teach his family the vocabulary words he was learning each day over the evening meal until the fires gave out.

"For much of the outside world," Bishop Gassis wrote in a February 19 call for a day of prayer for the Kauda victims,

> the young students of Kauda are war statistics. But for us, they are much more than that: They are our children whose struggle for education in the midst of war was itself a sign of extraordinary courage and hope.

But on a windswept hill in the Nuba Mountains, I heard something even simpler: A mourning father say as we parted company, "You understand that we will never leave here now, no matter what they [the regime] do to us. We will never leave the bones of our children to them."

IV

Max Picard once wrote that "the child is like a little hill of silence. . . . The word has difficulty in coming up from the silence of the child."[33]

Memorials to the death of children compound the difficulty Picard writes about, rising, as they must, not only out of the natural silence of childhood, but out of death's deeper, but no less speechless innocence.

Gustav Mahler, over his wife's superstitious objections, transformed Rückert's heart-broken *kindertotenlieder* into song in 1905, only to discover that the work, as his wife had feared, *did* presage the loss of their daughter, Marie, to scarlet fever two years later.

One cannot afford to make art out of the death of children.

If tribute is to be given, if it is to be proportionate to the nature of the loss, one suspects that the only adequate tribute to a child's death is the failure to rise to the occasion. If there is an appropriate word, it is the one that circles us back to the silence.

Memorials on the graves of children killed in war pose an even crueler dilemma, because the silences out of which they rise are criminal.

In Bosnia-Herzegovina, I nearly got myself run out of town once when it became generally known that I had ventured to the region's shadow side, a pit on a mountainside in a place called Surmanci. At the outset of World War II, the Croatian Catholic villagers of the area, in retaliation for Serbian attacks on local Catholic priests, had herded hundreds of Serbian Orthodox women and children up these slopes and buried them alive in a cave. After the war, victorious communist partisans erected a monumental obelisk on the site and made the locals pay for their sins with annual commemorations and decades of official reprisals.

I stumbled upon the place during Serbian excavations of the mass grave six months before the Balkan war started up in Croatia.

> We had reached the monument placed on the site in the '60s. The inscription abounded in communist pieties about "Ustashe crimes" (the Ustashe was the Croatian nationalist militia during the years of the Second World War) and Tito's victory over fascism. . . . "What exactly are you finding up there?" I asked [the leader of the dig] stupidly. He turned back, looking me over, and said, "Three meters of bones. Children's mostly."[34]

Four years later, as the Balkan war wore down, I took a fellow journalist with me to Surmanci. However, I couldn't seem to locate the site. The fifty-foot obelisk that once had made the children's grave visible for miles was nowhere to be seen. Eventually, we hiked up the flinty slope to what I guessed was the place, memorialized now only by mounds of dynamited rubble.

*   *   *

Kauda Foq, April 1, 2001

The idea for a memorial for the children of Kauda first arose during the walk back from visiting the families. War conditions had prevented large-scale gatherings to commemorate the children and local people felt that something should be done later, when conditions improved.

In addition, the schoolyard site had begun to inspire fear in the children. Classes, of course, were no longer held at the school; they were scattered throughout the area, in groves, to prevent them being spotted from the air. Nevertheless, children steered clear of the schoolyard, parents said, going out of their way to avoid crossing the gravel clearing still marked with bomb craters and blasted trees. Perhaps a memorial service of some kind could be arranged, a simple monument erected when the bishop was there, to redeem the place, to cleanse it of its associations.

A year later there was indeed a commemorative event at Kauda, but it was anything but a quiet local affair:

Press release
Diocese of El Obeid
April 8, 2001

US CATHOLIC DELEGATION TO SUDAN ERECTS
MEMORIAL TO 'MARTYRED' NUBA CHILDREN

In the middle of a sun-washed schoolyard in the Nuba Mountains, members of a high-level U.S. Catholic delegation lifted a six-foot-high metal cross over the site where twenty first-graders and their teacher died last year — victims of the Khartoum regime's bombing raids on civilian targets in southern and central Sudan.

The team dispatched to the Nuba Mountains on April 1 consisted of an American bishop, an African affairs advisor for the United States Catholic Conference (USCC), the bishops' policy arm, and two senior representatives of Catholic Relief Services (CRS), along with a contingent of support staff and journalists.

Bishop Edward Braxton of Lake Charles, La., a member of the international relations committee, headed up the two-day visit to mainly southern dioceses, Tambura, Yambio, Torit, Rumbek and Narus, which included the foray north to Nuba. Other members of the group traveling to the Nuba Mountains included Rev. Michael Perry, OFM, USCC policy adviser on African affairs, Mr. Ken Hackett, Executive Director of CRS, and Paul Townsend of CRS/Sudan, based in Nairobi.

Braving ninety-degree-plus temperatures and Khartoum's long-standing blockade of rebel-held areas of the Nuba Mountains, the team sought to spotlight US Catholic solidarity with these beleaguered communities, and conduct a brisk perusal of the parishes, schools and relief operations established here in recent years by the Diocese of El Obeid.

Given the military insecurity, they remained in the area just three hours.

Bishop Gassis, local priests, catechists, and diocesan personnel, along with new Governor Abdel Aziz el-Hilu, newly appointed civilian and military leader of non-government-controlled areas of the Nuba Mountains, greeted the delegation on arrival at the bush airstrip.

A relaxed, even festive atmosphere prevailed — this, despite the fact that airstrips are frequent targets of the regime's bombers and there is active fighting not far away in Heiban, the county seat. Large numbers of Nuba villagers, many in traditional tribal costumes, were on hand to welcome the delegation. And, in an unusual gesture, an honor guard of local Nuba defense forces under the authority of the Sudan People's Liberation Army (SPLA) mounted a sober military parade for the Americans.

And there were speeches. . . .[35]

*   *   *

The clearing in front of the primary school. A year ago, a scene of sudden terror, but today, the shady spot beside the sycamore, where the teacher and her students fell, had been transformed into a roadside shrine.

"God our Father, innocent children came here to this place, with their young teacher, eager to learn," Bishop Braxton intoned in the presence of villagers, school personnel, and more than two hundred schoolchildren who had survived the attack.

> They were Christian and Muslim children and children of traditional belief, united in a common future; on the morning of February 8 in the year 2000, here, beside this tree, they died.

Villagers and priests had erected a simple stepped stone and cement base, about the size of a child's tomb, to support the monumental cross. The impact crater, now bordered with bricks, was only feet away, a grim reminder of the sky-born terrors that still plague this region.

"From this place, insignificant to the world," Bishop Braxton went on in a prayer composed for the occasion,

Bombing site, schoolyard, Kauda, March 2000

You opened to them the gates of a larger life; in the wake of terror, you made their names known to the whole world, and, through them, drew the hearts of millions to this place. The blood of these martyrs is now joined with the sacrifice of your Son; their deaths a prayer for justice and a seed of the Gospel . . . Through their intercession, and the intercession of St. Bakhita, Mother of Sudan, deliver us from persecution and oppression, from slavery and all forms of violence.

The reference to Josephine Bakhita (1869-1947), the first Sudanese saint, canonized in October 2000, was apt. This former Sudanese slave who became an Italian religious hovers over this tragedy of children.

Born in eastern Sudan, Josephine Bakhita was captured by slave traders as a child. Her captors gave her the nickname "Bakhita," an Arabic name meaning "lucky." After being sold to Arab and Turkish masters, she was bought by an agent for the Italian consul in Khartoum, and was eventually taken as a domestic to Italy. In Venice she encountered the Canossian Sisters, and, through them, the Catholic faith. Bakhita was baptized in 1890. She took her vows as a Canossian Sister six years later. A fervent supporter of African missions, she never returned to Sudan. As the memorial inscription on the cross notes, the school attack took place on February 8, the anniversary of the saint's death, her feast day.

> In Memory of our Martyred
> Children and Teacher Killed
> At this spot
> On Feb. 8, 2000
> The anniversary of
> St. Bakhita's beatification
> Erected by
> Bishop John Richard [sic][36]
> And USCC Delegation
> On April 1st 2001.

Father Tom urged the Bakhita connection upon Catholics in Kauda during the first days after the attack:

> One really unique factor in all of this is that the day of the bombing was the feast of Bakhita. She died on February 8, 1947. I used this every time I preached and talked to the people. It seemed that it was some comfort and gave meaning to it all: Bakhita being there to receive the children into God's kingdom. The Sudanese Sister who was known for her love of children — I am sure that this is pretty much the way it happened.[37]

Today, a year later, the survivors of the attack, lined up on one side of the monument in crisp new uniforms, bore the self-possessed, inscrutable look Nuba children often project. It was hard to read their reactions.

They had made banners: "Yes to education, no to war," one read in English, doubtless for the delegation's benefit. Many of these bore crayon images of multi-colored bombers.

*   *   *

One could easily have missed the most eloquent gesture of the day. In fact, the speeches over at last, with vehicles to board and schedules to keep, some members of the delegation had already turned to go when two Nuba children, a girl and boy, both amputees, approached the monument.

Held in the arms of Bishop Gassis, Amani Hussien, her left arm a casualty of the attack, looked out at the scene with shy dignity. She lives with the Fathers now, helping out as she can, her family unable to provide for her, given her special needs. More recently, the lack of a prosthetic arm has caused her posture to list, harbinger, one fears, of far greater disabilities to come.

Absently at first, the girl put her left hand into a bowl of flower petals, and then, turning back to look over her shoulder at the place where the terror had struck, began to drop white petals one at a time over the smooth stone surface beneath the tree.

CHAPTER 6

Early Rains

Please pray with all your heart for the situation in the Nuba Mountains. The darkest hour has come. . . .

Ferdinand von Habsburg,
e-mail to the author, May 25, 2001

Nuba soldiers, April 2001

On March 31, 2001, Yusuf Kuwa Mekki, SPLM governor of Southern Kordofan, died in a London hospital of bone cancer. After obsequies in Nairobi, he was buried in the Nuba Mountains on April 10. Kuwa (1945-2001) was only in his mid-fifties, but few doubted that his death marked the end of an era in the political resurgence of the Nuba people.

Perhaps more than any other single figure, Kuwa summed up in his own life the experience of a whole generation of university-educated Nuba, the young men of Komolo and other mid-century Nuba political movements who laid the groundwork for the SPLA-led insurgency in southern Kordofan.

Born into an assimilated Nuba family, Kuwa said that he believed himself to be an Arab until secondary school.

> That is what we were taught. As I understood what was happening and became politically conscious, I recognized that I was Nuba, not Arab.[1]

Kuwa, who often referred to himself as a "free-thinking" Muslim, went on to get a degree in political science from the University of Khartoum. At university, ill at ease in his world, he explored African literature and political thought, particularly the writings of Tanzania's Julius Nyerere, and discovered the proud history of the Nuba.

> I remember since elementary school until I went to the university that there was nothing in the history books about the Nuba that was good. It was only about how the Turks came to Sudan and brought slaves from the Nuba Mountains and the South. So, in these books, we are always slaves. . . . One day I went to Khartoum library and I started to look into Sudan section, and I asked myself: "Why don't I search about things written about the Nuba?" . . . I found many books inside that library about the Nuba and their origins. Now came a big question, "Why are not we taught about this in our schools?" . . . The conclusion, of course, was that there is something wrong in Sudan that must be corrected. And this question of Sudan being an Arab country really is the wrong basis on which Sudanism is built. With this in mind, I started to think, we have to do something.[2]

In Khartoum, Kuwa joined other Nuba students in political and social debates, eventually founding, along with friends Daniel Kodi, Abdel Aziz el-Hilu and others, a clandestine youth organization dedicated to raising Nuba cultural awareness. Komolo, the organization's name, means "youth" in the Miri and Kadugli languages, a vivid indication that the group rejected the compromises with northern assimilationist policies that an older generation of Nuba politicians was prepared to make:[3]

> To me being Nuba means to be a human being, with dignity and identity.[4]

Kuwa returned to Kadugli as a schoolteacher and, determined to work within the system, went into politics, where, against all odds, he won a seat in the Regional Assembly in 1981.

However, what should have been an opportunity for Nuba to gain political influence in provincial affairs was quickly foiled both by competing local Arab interests and by divisions among the Nuba parties themselves.[5]

In 1983, President Nimeiri imposed Islamic *shari'a* law on the country and abrogated the 1972 Addis Ababa Agreement, setting Sudan on a path to renewed civil war. By 1984, Kuwa had given up on regional politics and opted, with other Komolo associates, to join the southern-led Sudan People's Liberation Army to fight for a secular Sudan.

> Why the SPLA? The SPLA program referred to a New Sudan for all Sudanese, not just for southerners. Garang spoke of unity on the basis of free choice, unity with decentralization. . . . Most Nuba support the SPLA, though a few resent the inadequate support the Nuba receive from the South. . . . My role in the Convention, I believe, educated many in the SPLM. Our voice in the [SPLM] was loud, and the Convention's resolutions clearly identified the Nuba as part of the SPLM's vision.[6]

He entered the Nuba Mountains in 1989 at the head of the New Kush Battalion, which spearheaded the establishment of an SPLA base of operations in the eastern *jebels*. Though not the most gifted military strat-

egist among the top SPLA commanders, Kuwa was the inspiration behind the founding of the South Kordofan Advisory Council, popularly
known as the Nuba parliament, in 1992, which, in the midst of catastrophic military defeats, pioneered the creation of a civilian infrastructure in rebel-held zones that significantly boosted popular Nuba support for the insurgency and for the SPLA.

As British journalist Julie Flint, a longtime Kuwa supporter, said of
him:

> He led by example. In the mountains, cut off from the world, he
> showed a concern for human rights that was, and is, unequalled in
> any rebel group — not least of all the SPLA, which has a deplorable
> record of brutality in southern Sudan. He was the first SPLA com-
> mander to permit independent human rights monitoring, the first to
> set up a civil administration, the only one to support a judiciary that
> was sufficiently confident to bring soldiers to court.[7]

I met him only once, in his Nairobi office, shortly after the Kauda
bombing, and not under the best of circumstances.

From my journal:

> To Yusuf Kuwa's office on a side street in an nondescript Nairobi
> neighborhood. Not the sort of place one brings the "quality" to; a
> gray suite of rooms the color of cigarettes for journalists and
> midlevel bureaucrats. All the public emblems, the SPLA flag, the of-
> ficial photos have been bleached by long exposure to the Kenyan sun.
> From the look of it, real business gets done here.

Ferdinand von Habsburg, the bishop's relief coordinator, and I had a
meeting with Walid Hamed, the governor's aide, about passes to the
Nuba Mountains and other paperwork. For the first time, the governor's office was charging fees for arranging SPLA travel documents to
the Nuba Mountains.

Can't be a lucrative business at this stage, I couldn't help thinking.

Kuwa joined us, sliding into a chair behind the large official desk
that took up most of the room.

I had heard that there were tensions between the governor and the bishop's office. A not unusual state of affairs, as I'd come to learn, "differences" between SPLM authorities and church leaders in rebel-held zones.

In southern Sudan, these "tensions" tended to range from human rights violations, such as forcible recruitment of lay workers into the SPLA and the enlistment of child soldiers, to looting of church property by soldiers and detention of church personnel.[8] Between Gassis and the governor's office, the tensions seemed more personal.

Ferdinand, eager to improve relations, told Kuwa about the progress of ambitious diocesan water projects in the Nuba Mountains. I had been given the task of briefing the governor on the bishop's recent diplomatic triumphs in the United States, the Wilberforce Award, the meeting with Secretary of State Madeleine Albright, and so on.

Already a very sick man, Kuwa closed his eyes and interrupted the recital in a low voice: "We are well aware of who the bishop is, and what he is doing for us."

I searched the governor's expression for a hint of irony; but the only thing one could read on his face with certainty was weariness.

Kuwa's body was flown to Kenya where the Nuba leader was mourned by the large expatriate Sudanese community there in a week of private and public ceremonies, including an SPLA tribute at a Nairobi sports stadium, before being buried in the Nuba Mountains.

Flint relates that the rumor was spread that Kuwa would be buried near the graves of the victims of the Kauda bombing; an impossibility, given the fact that the children were buried near their family compounds. As it turned out, it was a ruse put out to mislead Khartoum's agents, who were already showing an alarming degree of interest in the precise location of the rebel leader's tomb.

Flint, who was present at the funeral in Luere, the SPLA military headquarters south of Kauda, relates that Kuwa

> was buried in military uniform without his stripes, the way he liked to dress among his men. There were many tributes . . . And then it was over. The coffin was lowered into a deep grave and covered with aluminum sheeting and cement set with handles. If government

Nuba honor guard, April 2001

forces ever advance on the area, the cement can be removed and [Kuwa's body] carried to safety.

II

Everything had gone wrong that morning. Radio operators indicated that the plane sent from Lokichokio to pick up the bishop and his team would arrive ahead of schedule. Quartered in Gidel, east of the airstrip, we would have to hurry if we wanted to make the flight. In addition, Bishop Gassis had arranged to meet with the new governor, Abdel Aziz, on the tarmac, a procedure that would mean further delays at the landing strip.

Everyone was jumpy. For one thing, government bombers had been hovering over the area the previous day, Easter Sunday, dropping ordnance on a site near Lumon. We were sure they would return. With high-level delegations going and coming from Nairobi, with a growing and disciplined SPLA presence in the region, and a few NGOs at least willing to explore the possibility of defying the government's ban on aid to rebel-held areas, let alone Gassis's provocative visits, government reprisals, in the form of bombing raids, would predictably increase.

Fortunately, it was approaching the point of no return for large-scale dry season offensives in the Nuba Mountains, we thought. The murderous heat wave roiling central Sudan pointed to the early onset of the rainy season, locals said, making it unlikely that government garrisons would risk big mechanized assaults until the fall.

I had never seen such weather. Intense heat and the Nuba Mountains went together in my experience, especially in April; but added to the 110-degree temperatures was a rising humidity that made it almost difficult to breathe.

On top of that, to the dust that normally built up in the valleys at the end of the dry season, one had to add smoke and ash from the hundreds of brush fires Nuba farmers had lit on the slopes, burning off the grassland in preparation for planting.

Outdoors, sitting in a circle under the sky in what we had long ago dubbed "the parliament," night after night, we watched the hillsides burn.

*   *   *

And we had the new land cruiser to worry about.

It was the first vehicle in this part of the eastern *jebels,* if you discount the diocese's two motorbikes, which, due to frequent mishaps, were rarely mobile. Even the military had no such equipment.

A note from my journal:

Driving with the bishop from a meeting with Abdel Aziz, cheerfully deflowering the terrain. Local Nuba have, on the bishop's instructions, cleared brush from the main footpaths, allowing the land cruiser to plow them into roads. When in doubt, despite the age-old

158

Women on path, morning, Nuba Mountains

counsel of walkers, we create our own, sending rabbits scurrying in
terror into the underbrush and the livestock, who've never seen such
a great white-eyed beast before, bellowing out of our way. Since
Nuba graves are often situated near, or even in the middle of footpaths, I find myself in the delicate position of trying to keep the
bishop, barreling at full tilt, from running into, worse, over them. As
for the people, whenever they see the car, they stand aside, the
women ululating in astonished approval.

I couldn't help but recall poet Wendell Berry's analysis, in his agrarian
essays, that the path is the form and the enactment of a relationship
with a landscape.

"A path is little more than a habit that comes with knowledge of a place," Berry writes,

> It is a form of contact with a known landscape. It is not destructive . . . [I]t obeys the natural contours; such obstacles as it meets, it goes around. A road, on the other hand, even the most primitive road, embodies a resistance against the landscape. Its reason is not simply the necessity for movement, but haste. Its wish is to *avoid* contact with the landscape. . . Its form is the form of speed, dissatisfaction and anxiety.[9]

Speed might not be the operative word in our case since, although we were certainly pioneering the Kauda-Gidel traffic grid, we kept getting the land cruiser stuck in the sandy bottoms of dry washes. Happily, we could always count on the local camel drivers to figure out a way to set us free.

*   *   *

"It would have been more efficient to *walk*," I said to the bishop as we pulled up to the Buffalo cargo plane that, as predicted, had already arrived, and had time to park at the far end of the airstrip, piloted by a crew that, by now, had also run out of patience.

The land cruiser, again: laden with visitors, soldiers, and luggage, spinning its wheels in river sand all the way to the landing strip.

"We've got to get out of here," the manager of the transport service complained, mindful not only of the war, but of other relief flights that were due to arrive that morning.

Gassis, in the meantime, had gone off, as planned, to have a brisk meeting with Abdel Aziz and other commanders in a burned-out shell of a building in the scrub brush a short distance from the airstrip.

The bishop and I had joined the new governor at this same spot a few days before, where there had been sugared tea, goat butchered for the occasion, and, courtesy of the new commander, the snappiest military salutes I had ever received in the Nuba Mountains.

A surprisingly gentle, thoughtful man for a career soldier, Abdel Aziz Adam el-Hilu, with Kuwa one the founders of Komolo and the Nuba political underground, had arrived in the region with a reputation

Dinka cattle crossing the Loll River, northern Bahr al-Ghazal

for integrity, but, more to the point, for skill, even brilliance as an SPLA military strategist.

"Something must really be going to happen," a Nuba had told me, "if they're sending a man like that here."

Though El-Hilu's ancestors hail from Dar Masalit in Darfur, he is considered "assimilated to the Nuba." His formal remarks welcoming the American Catholic delegation a few weeks before made his allegiances clear:

> The problem of the Nuba people is considered as a microcosm for the problems of the marginalized people in other parts of the Sudan.

The only difference, perhaps, is that the Nuba people have historically endured more oppression and marginalization than any other group in the Sudan, and they have resisted all attempts at ethnic cleansing and cultural assimilation by the Arabo-Islamic center for the last two hundred years, when the Turko-Egyptian colonialists created the current-day Sudan, with its current political geographical borders in 1821.[10]

He led the first SPLA units to enter the Nuba Mountains in 1987, the so-called Volcano Battalion, which successfully organized large-scale recruitment for the SPLA in the region until Kuwa's New Kush Battalion advanced into the *jebels* two years later. By the mid-1990s, he was serving as head of logistics at SPLA headquarters in Nairobi.[11]

Weeks earlier, I had gotten a sense of the man when, in the back of the land cruiser, with soldiers and members of the American Catholic delegation, Abdel Aziz had borne with equanimity the recital of a foreign official's Sudan qualifications and thorough grasp of the situation.

"Yes," the commander responded wistfully, "when we started this campaign in 1983, we said, 'It won't be like *Anyanya*,[12] it won't go on forever. Five years at most,' we said, 'five years for the New Sudan.' Look at us now," he laughed. "Eighteen years later, *longer* than *Anyanya*, and still no end in sight."

With the bishop occupied with the governor, and Jim Nicholls snapping a few last shots of a soldier guarding the airstrip, I joined diocesan personnel, Nuba porters, and the flight crew tossing luggage and boxes into the rear cargo hold of the plane.

I suppose it was because the land cruiser's motor was still running that I didn't hear the Antonov.

Suddenly, out of nowhere, without a sound, the Nuba around me flattened themselves on the ground with the precision of a well-practiced drill. I followed suit just in time to hear a string of thudding explosions from the direction of the far end of the runway — four, five, six concussions. The ground shuddered beneath me, the air electric with the smell of cordite, like the scent of new sweat.

A later note, written while the experience was still fresh in the nerves:

In a moment like that everything has "edges," everything is "edged," as if, in an instant, one has cubist eyes, seeing everything from every angle at once because every shape one sees has acquired the potential to harm.

I looked up: Six plumes of dust in the direction of the mosque, not five hundred feet from the plane.

Nuba porters, diocesan personnel, soldiers, travelers angling for seats, all scattered for safety. To add to the confusion, the other relief flight scheduled to arrive that morning, on final approach to the airstrip, saw the barrel bombs fall, and had to take diversionary action to avoid the besieged field.

Gassis, meanwhile, with the commanders, had heard the Antonov. "One of the soldiers said, 'Look,' pointing to the plane," the bishop related. "Then, all of a sudden, he cried, 'O my God, they've dropped them,' meaning the bombs, and we all, Abdel Aziz, myself and the others, just fell flat."

That's when the *commedia* began.

Our pilot, wishing, understandably, to get into the air before the bomber could turn for another sortie, corralled his dazed passengers into their seats and started immediate preparations for departure.

Not before I had concluded, however, on the basis of a pilot's misapprehended shout, that we were evacuating the plane. (Perhaps the Antonov had reappeared above the landing strip, I thought.) And out I jumped. Imagine my surprise when, instead of seeing my fellow passengers scurrying down the ladder behind me, I heard the plane door slam and a propeller start.

The pilot's shout had been intended for a hapless SPLA bureaucrat who had boarded the plane to check papers. The captain had had too many delays for one morning, especially when the next one might be permanent.

Outside, with the plane preparing to taxi, I must admit that it did occur to me for a split second that remaining behind in the Nuba Mountains was an option; and then I dashed around to the cargo door on the other side of the fuselage and began to pound.

Doors slid open, hands reached out as the plane began to roll down the runway and, as the bishop is fond of describing it, the captain hauled me into the plane "like a sack of potatoes."

A minute later, we were off the ground, and, after a tense moment, checking to see that we were clear of returning Antonovs and diverted relief flights, nosed into the open sky.

Press Release
April 17, 2001

KHARTOUM ATTACKS BISHOP'S PLANE
IN NUBA MOUNTAINS

April 16, Kauda, Sudan — Sudanese airforce bombers attacked an airstrip in the remote Nuba Mountains Monday, narrowly missing a plane carrying Bishop Macram Max Gassis of El Obeid diocese in central Sudan. The bishop, long time champion of Sudan's marginalized peoples, was making his Easter pastoral visit to rural parishes here on the frontlines of Sudan's 18-year-old civil war.

The bishop and his entourage escaped unhurt, but, according to the latest reports, one Nuba militiaman was killed and two civilians seriously injured in the mid-morning attack on the airfield by a Russian-made Antonov bomber. . . This was the second attack in as many days in the Nuba Mountains . . . Late reports indicate that the bombers continued their assault today with a series of random bombings in the Kauda area.

The Easter Monday bombing at the Kauda airstrip marks the most serious attack yet on the Church leader and veteran human rights spokesman. In 1998, Khartoum-sponsored bombing raids marred Gassis-led Christmas festivities in the Nuba Mountains. This past Christmas, Antonovs pelted Kauda, site of yesterday's incident, with barrel bombs on Dec. 23, forcing the bishop to delay his plans to visit the region.

Gassis may not have been the only target of Monday's bombing. Among the local dignitaries seeing the Churchman off were the new SPLA governor of Southern Kordofan, Abdel Aziz el-Hilu, whose organizational skills are already having an effect on the region's morale and the cohesion of its military forces.[13]

Four days after the bombing, in an April 20 *Agence France Presse* report, Sudanese army spokesman Gen. Mohamed Beshir Suleiman denied that government air force bombers attacked the Nuba Mountains on April 16. He called the allegations "baseless."

There was silence in the plane as we flew by a route that I, for one, had never taken, over the scar the vast oil fields of Bentiu make in the plains of Upper Nile.

"[T]he oil discoveries in Bentiu," Abdel Aziz had told the American delegation days before,

> have had a negative impact . . . on the Nuba people. The pipeline taking oil to Port Sudan for export passes through the area [southeastern Nuba Mountains] and the NIF regime decided to wipe out all the population who happened to have been sitting along that line ever since time immemorial. . . . It is extermination and scorched earth policy that is taking place. Their intention is to widen the security zone for the oil to pass without consideration to human lives. We lost hundreds of civilians who were killed and over 40,000 people displaced between March 2000 and January 2001 just because of this oil.[14]

Two hours later, we landed safely in Turalei, northern Bahr al-Ghazal.

III

It wasn't until well after dark that the bishop, Jim Nicholls, the Sisters, and myself, huddled at one end of an acacia-wood fire against the mosquitoes, spoke for the first time about what had happened that morning.

The two Comboni Missionary Sisters had been part of the entourage since we left Nairobi. Sister Gianfranca Silvestri, the congregation's provincial for South Sudan, and the younger Sister Anna Gastaldello, who was then based at Mariallou in Bahr al-Ghazal, had come to the Nuba Mountains to assess what the Comboni Missionary Sisters could do to assist the pastoral work there. Sister Anna, along with other Comboni Sisters, later helped spearhead the establishment of a convent in Gidel.

The talk was quiet, halting, as if each of us was held back by a need not to hinder the freedom of the others. Close calls, I've learned, are like that: To know precisely what happened, or from what one has managed to escape becomes a matter not of curiosity but of need; each detail, however insignificant, the smallest fragment of fact or perspective vital, as if the event itself cannot take shape until every one of its pieces is accounted for.

The Sisters, not surprisingly, were less focused on the threat to themselves than on what the attack revealed about the stark predicament of the people. "To know something by hearsay is one thing," Sister Gianfranca told me,

> but to live with this music of the Antonov, to see these poor people who live there, the children growing up, living in the shadow of death. Until when will this continue? Pray for them, yes, but the world must do something for these people. . . You are there, the bombs are falling, the fear and the panic. The people are really struggling, the lack of rain, poor agriculture, but then you add this terror. Even beasts would not do this! At the time, I think, well, let us stay with the bishop and die with him.[15]

"It was very sad," added Sister Anna. "The people, though, didn't look afraid. It's as if they're saying, what can we do, there's no safe place for us."[16]

*　　*　　*

The insufferably hot night made trying to sleep indoors, in the squat, windowless huts out of the question. Iron beds were hauled out under the sky, sleeping bags unrolled, mosquito mesh strung from overhanging branches. Eventually, flashlights in hand, we settled in for the night.

I found myself relieved somehow that we were all together, that I could still account for everyone, scattered though we were about the compound, each in his or her muslin cocoon, reading or listening to the short wave or asleep — in a few instances, all three.

Sleep: There was little chance of that in my case.

Lying on my back staring at the sky, I found myself rehearsing the morning raid again and again, going over every inch of it like a surveyor.

The usual quandaries:

The soldier who was reported killed in the attack was he the one I'd talked to at the perimeters of the airfield the one I'd thought about but hadn't asked to help us load the cargo if he was the one and I think he was would he still be alive if I'd asked him. . .

After what seemed like hours, I forced myself to stop. Nothing of what had happened, I told myself, not a single word, not even a breath of it could be repealed. Finality: the consummation of regrets.

I recalled that in the weeks before traveling to Sudan this time, I had had two experiences, premonitions, if you like, while walking to the supermarket. They were such unusual, insistent sensations that I actually took notes on an old envelope I had in my pocket. Later, of course, little of what I had jotted down *in situ* made any sense at all.

Beginning suddenly, out of the blue, one day: the sensation, more, a *recall* of quite specific smells, the precise "feeling" associated with certain weather patterns, the character of light in places I've lived in the past, as if they, or intimations of them were present to me as I went about my daily activities. This, unbidden, went on for days.

A night or so later, as I walked to the market at dusk, a moment of intellectual clarity about the "theme" of my life, the insight for which my life had been lived, what it was for.

The Repentant Affirmation: One made without exclusion,
    and from within
Unity
This is the truth that justified my life.

From the notes written on the envelope:

Tonight:
The unity of all my places
Worlds meshing (coming together)
(discreet)

not forms of loss (nostalgia)
(there is no loss)

I carry about [in] me all my places.

Confiding the experience to a few friends, I joked that, while grateful, I worried that such "epiphanies" come to people only when they're about to die.

*   *   *

I awoke with a start just before dawn. I had drifted off to sleep after all.

The fires were out. No one stirred in the compound. The air was thick with moisture and a vanguard of sharp breezes. Dark cloudbanks on either side of the field of vision rippled with lightning, and I could already feel the first droplets of rain.

Straight above me was a prodigy: between the two flashing cloud banks, on the verge of closing, a river of clear open sky, black as the mind of a god, through which a brilliant late summer moon was sailing.

I gave wordless, untranslatable thanks and lay back to welcome the rain.

Two weeks later, the government of Sudan, invading on multiple fronts, launched the largest single military operation in the Nuba Mountains in a decade.

IV

5/25/01

. . . The situation in the Nuba Mountains has become critical. . . . Government soldiers have broken into the Heiban region from several directions (east — Umdurdu and south — Kalkada). The fighting around the airstrips has spread to Kauda Foq and Gidel areas.

As of one hour ago, the Fathers are in the bush outside their compounds with radio operating. The situation could not be worse. We are trying to see how to evacuate them out. The governor's office (Walid) are trying their best to contain the situation and to organize the evacuation of people, but it seems that even that is not possible under the circumstances. Fighting is all around. . . . All the Fathers are fine. Abraham, George and Isaac are in the Kauda area, while Solomon and Joseph are in Gidel. Kauda communicates by radio while Gidel with SAT phone. . . . They have no way to join each other right now.

The SPLA position is desperately tight. There is artillery shelling every where. . . . Solomon says that SPLA soldiers have surrendered in some places but the fighting continues unabated all around. He is with soldiers protecting him. There are reports that Chauri, Umdurdu and Karga have been burnt totally. We cannot move any plane and the situation remains unclear where the advantage lies. Our people are in great danger, without a doubt.

Bishop, I don't know what to tell you except we need to pray. All your work may be to no avail unless our people are safe and SPLA can somehow push back the enemy. . . .

Ferdinand

The attack caught everyone by surprise. The perennial "dry season" offensives normally began in February or March; long before the region's torrential rainy season gave the military advantage to guerillas. With the onset of early rains, it appeared unlikely that government forces would try to mount a full-scale attack on the Nuba Mountains, but would be forced to limit themselves to "combing" operations and aerial bombardment until the fall.

Then, in the early morning hours of May 22, 2001, six government convoys armed with heavy artillery and rocket launchers attacked rebel-held territory from five directions. The mission: to clear rebel troops from Heiban county, their last sizable stronghold, and thus, for all practical purposes, break the back of Nuba resistance in the region.

Code-named "The Heroes of Adar Yel," after the place where a dozen high-level government military officers died in an air crash April 4, the offensive, involving more than 7,000 troops, constituted the largest single military engagement since the Tullishi campaign of 1992, in which more than 40,000 government forces were beaten back by the SPLA.

The late May offensive, at least at the outset, was not going nearly that well. During the ten days of heavy fighting, SPLA troops, despite the considerable military skill of their commander, spent much of it in retreat. Gaining the upper hand by May 26, SPLA forces mounted a counteroffensive and, in a bold maneuver, captured the government garrison of Umm Sardiba on May 27. Government forces were in full retreat by early June.

Father Joseph Moga, a young Sudanese priest, was there.

Q: You were stationed in Gidel parish, right?

Father Joseph: Yes, I came in the year 2000 for my pastoral year, which was to end in 2001 with the renewal of my vows [as a religious].

Q: When did the fighting start?

A: It began in stages. The war started in early to mid-May, but it intensified in late May, and that is when we had to abandon the parish [in Gidel].

Q: How did you come to that conclusion?

A: The Sudan government army was so close to us, so we had to abandon the parish and move to Kauda. Those fellows were just too close. They took one of the mountains near us.

Q: Which mountain?

A: Kumu. So we had to move out.

Q: What was that experience like?

A: The experience was so hard because we had to maneuver our way out through the mountains, to make sure that we were safe, in order to reach Kauda. So we went on foot with the Fathers and some Christians were with us carrying those items that we decided to take with us, that were too important to leave behind to be destroyed there.

Q: When did you make the decision to move?

A: In the morning hours. We left with our guards, with the [SPLA] soldiers who were given to us by the governor [Abdel Aziz] to make sure that they take care of the priests and we left the parish under SPLA guard. Then we went to Kauda.

Q: How did you manage to avoid the fighting?

A: There were some youths who showed us the roads that were passable, that we could use to avoid the militias and where the fighting was taking place. They were staying on the tops of hills so they could watch everything. So we went and safely reached the parish in Kauda.

Q: Do you think that the parishes were military objectives for the government troops?

A: Yes, these two parishes were targets because in one way or another they were helping the people to stay. People could not get all these [relief] items if the parishes weren't there. So that was one of their aims, to make sure they captured these places and demolished them, all the things we were doing which were sustaining the people.

Q: What about the land cruiser that was in Gidel? What did you do with it?

A: The land cruiser we had to take to a certain valley, hard to get to, and cover it with some leaves so that nobody could see it. Later on, we were afraid that these guys [government of Sudan soldiers] could push further, so we organized the [SPLA] soldiers and had to maneuver a way to bring the land cruiser to Kauda. So, in fact, the journey took a whole day, cutting trees, looking for a place where you can drive and not be noticed -

Q: Risky.

A: Very dangerous. Around 5:30 that's when we entered the parish (Kauda). Everybody was joyful because now the car these fellows were longing for is safe. People were happy. That was maybe May 31. When the first of June came, we started preparing for the renewal of my vows. By now the fear had gone away. We thought, if we stayed all this time alive, I think God will protect us.

Q: What about evacuation? Was that ever an option you considered?

A: The governor told us, if things get really tough then the priests could be evacuated, because some of the NGO personnel were being evacuated. But we said, no, because if we go, I think things will become tough even for you people [in the military], because our presence will encourage you and give you morale to defend the people. Then everybody remained firm. Seeing the priests, seeing Christ's presence among them, people believed eventually this war will end. That's what encouraged the people, in fact, to push on.

Q: How *did* the fighting end?

A: To our surprise, on June 4, in the morning hours, there was no gunshot. We waited to get the news. Eventually, in the evening somebody told us, we believe these fellows have left. Then came June 5, the real news came, from reliable sources, these fellows left, they couldn't continue any more. Then, of course, on the sixth, we moved back to Gidel. Everybody came to cheer. Then our life came back.

Q: What would have happened, do you think, if the government campaign had succeeded?

A: If it had succeeded, it would have been real tough for the movement to exist probably within the Nuba area, because this is where the late Yusuf Kuwa was buried.

Q: Was his grave also a target, do you think?

A: Yes, also a target. If they could have succeeded in capturing the place, we don't know what they would have done to the grave of this man.

According to the SPLA, more than 8,000 homes were destroyed during the offensive, dozens of civilians killed or wounded, and thousands displaced by the fighting.[17]

Despite the losses, the collapse of the government's 2001 dry season campaign against the SPLA in Heiban county proved decisive. It was the last battle in Khartoum's sixteen-year war against the Nuba.

By early November 2001, five months after the end of the offensive, Senator John Danforth, the Bush Administration's Special Envoy for Peace in the Sudan, was meeting with officials in Khartoum to broker the terms for a cease-fire in the Nuba Mountains. Far from a "separate peace," Danforth's hope was that the Nuba agreement would, in addition to relieving frontline populations of the worst aspects of the war, provide a test-case for confidence-building measures between the government and the SPLA. Should the Nuba agreement succeed, the argument ran, it would lay the groundwork for other localized cease-fire arrangements and, eventually for a permanent, comprehensive settlement of Africa's longest civil war.

The provisions of the cease-fire agreement, with its call for security, access to humanitarian aid and cessation of aerial bombardment, harked back, at least in part, to proposals floated by Gassis and Sudan's Catholic bishops in the last years of the war. I myself was present, along with William Saunders, when the bishop presented a six-point proposal, with a Nuba cease-fire as its centerpiece, to Secretary of State Colin Powell that spring.

Danforth returned to Khartoum in mid-November to press the government on preparations for the cease-fire.[18] And two months later, on January 19, 2002, the Nuba Mountains Cease-Fire Agreement (CFA) was signed at the Swiss resort of Burgenstock by Commmander Abdel Aziz el-Hilu, for the Sudan People's Liberation Movement/Nuba, and Dr. Mutrif Saddiq Ali, for the government of the Republic of Sudan. U.S., Norwegian, and Swiss officials were on hand to witness the signing.

Among the principles established by the ceasefire:

> . . . the cessation of hostilities between the Parties in the Nuba Mountains;
>
> . . . the free movement of civilians and goods, including humanitarian assistance, throughout the Nuba Mountains;
>
> . . . the cessation of . . . hostilities, military movements, including reconnaissance and reinforcements, as well as hostile actions; all attacks by air or land, as well as acts of sabotage and the laying of mines; attempts to occupy new ground positions and movement of troops and resources . . .; all acts of violence against or other abuse of the civilian population, e.g., summary executions, torture, harassment, arbitrary detention and persecution of civilians on the basis of ethnic origin, religion or political affiliations, incitement of ethnic hatred, . . . use of child soldiers, sexual violence, training of terrorists, genocide and the bombing of the civilian population.[19]

Needless to say, the Nuba agreement was greeted with considerable skepticism by many foreign Sudan activists as well as by elements within the SPLM itself. Khartoum's agreement to humanitarian cease-fires in the South, from which the Nuba Mountains had been typically excluded, had been a feature of the war, resulting all too often in the freeing-up of government troops for redeployment on other fronts.

But, to everyone's surprise, the Nuba not least of all, the ceasefire, despite violations and setbacks, held.

As Andreas Vogt has noted, that the agreement held was due, in part, to war fatigue on both sides but, more importantly, to the presence of international monitors.

> [I]n a time where 'successful' is a rare description of peace efforts applied to African conflicts, [I wish to] highlight one of the few fairly prosperous peace mission arrangements going on in Africa today — namely, the Joint Monitoring Mission (JMM) and, more specifically, the Joint Military Commission's (JMC) implementation of the so-called Nuba Mountains cease-fire agreement (CFA).[20]

The JMC, composed of representatives from each party to the conflict as well as international representatives, has, among the terms of its mandate, verifying compliance with the provisions of the ceasefire, supervising the clearing of landmines, and resolving disputes. A Norwegian brigadier-general chairs the JMC.

"There are several aspects of the commission that make it . . . unique," Vogt adds:

> First of all, it is not mandated by the UN, as most international peace initiatives are today — especially if it involves military troops on the ground. . . . The JMC is supported politically by the so-called Friends of the Nuba Mountains, . . . composed of several diplomats based in Khartoum, representing the countries sponsoring the Joint Monitoring Mission, including numerous European countries, Canada and the US.[21]

*   *   *

Despite the talk of peace, however, as the year 2001 neared its end, the war, it seemed, was not quite over.

A squad sent from the government garrison of Heiban assassinated Agostino el-Nur Ibrahim, Bishop Gassis's catechist, on Nov. 19, 2001. The attack occurred during a temporary "good faith" cease-fire in the region that Danforth had negotiated with the government. El-Nur, a local magistrate, along with several other community leaders, was killed in his home near Kumu.

I last saw Agostino in Gidel during that memorable Easter of 1999. We sat next to each other at a *sibr* ceremony after Mass that afternoon. It was a time of relative peace — there hadn't been aerial bombardment in that part of the *jebels* for a month or so — and people were more relaxed than I had seen them.

Agostino was not working as a catechist in those days, but as a judicial officer for the civil administration. He was doing important work, not only adjudicating cases but helping in the monumental task of codifying customary law in the Nuba Mountains, trying to marshal the mostly unwritten Nuba tribal codes into a workable legal system.

As the festivities wound down at dusk, drums in the distance announced the arrival of visitors. No one on the reviewing stand seemed to know who they might be; the civil administration officials were there, all the local Catholics, people from the nearby villages.

The drummers turned out to be a group of Muslim Nuba who had come to pay their respects. "Sufis," people said. Dressed in traditional Sudanese caftans, they chanted the name "Allah," lifting Korans above their heads, moving in a kind of round dance as they saluted their neighbors on the occasion of the Christian feast.

One of the commanders, clearly moved, turned to me and said, "This is why we're fighting, you know, this is what it's all about!"

And then I remembered Agostino.

The catechist had been imprisoned and tortured in the early years of the war in an attempt to make him convert.

"I was working as a catechist in Lubi in the Nuba Mountains," Agostino told me when I interviewed him in 1998.

I was arrested there on April 14, 1985 and taken to Heiban. I spent one week there under torture. They tied me up with ropes and chains and beat me, there were lashings. Quit being a Christian, they said, and close your church. After that, I was transferred to Kadugli. The conditions there were worse. Christianity is not the religion for Sudan, they said, it's a religion for foreigners. What have you got to do with this religion of infidels? Others said, Repent, if you die, you'll leave your children fatherless. One officer offered me money and a house in Khartoum if I would change my religion. I was tortured there for four months, deprived of food and water for days, hoisted up, spat upon and beaten, my genitals pulled with pliers, my beard pulled out.

Failing to convert the catechist, prison guards tied him to the ground in a cross-like formation, a kind of mock crucifixion.

How I managed to get out of their hands, I still don't know. It was a kind of miracle.[22]

Even now, more than ten years later, el-Nur could talk about the experience only with great difficulty. In fact, when I interviewed him, only the bishop had seemed able to get him to tell me what had happened.

I turned to see what Agostino made of the Muslims' *sibr* gesture.

But he was not with the other elders. When I finally located him, Agostino was in the middle of the circle, dancing there with the Sufis.

CHAPTER 7

Notes on the Borders of Peace

How Sin Came into the World

There was a woman with two calabashes, one good, one bad.

It so happened that someone came and asked for water. But the calabashes of good and evil were both full. So the woman poured the contents of one of the calabashes into the other. She then had a calabash free to fill with water to quench her neighbor's thirst.

But then she realized what she had done. "I have mixed the good with the bad," she cried. "How am I going to separate them again?" Try as she might, she could not now purify the calabashes, nor prevent the good from being always mixed with bad, nor the bad mixed with good.

A Nuba story told to the author,
December 1998

Signing of the Permanent Truce, Naivasha, Kenya, 2005

On more than one occasion, I have been present when wars ended. In at least one instance, I had the chance to return two or three years later to see what survivors had made of the peace.

In Bosnia the war had ground to a halt with vague talk of the need for communal reconciliation — at least between Croats and Muslims, former allies who had turned on each other as the Balkan war progressed. At that time, I had asked a hardheaded Croatian friend, who had brought up the subject (much to my surprise), to tell me what he thought reconciliation between the warring parties might involve.

He thought for a moment, and said, "Christians should raise money to rebuild the mosques we destroyed, and Muslims should rebuild our churches — that would be a start."

Such generosity wasn't likely in any case, but two years later when I returned to the region, it had hardened into impossibility.

"Why would you want to strengthen your enemy?" the same friend remarked when I reminded him of his earlier views. Faced with daunting political challenges, the region, I soon discovered, had, like my friend, retreated into political apathy and the *cul-de-sac* of tribal and clan exclusivities.

It was with some trepidation, then, that I returned to Sudan in the last weeks of 2004.

*   *   *

Bishop Gassis's relief coordinator, Roberto Bronzino, summed up the situation nicely when I interviewed him the day before we flew to the Nuba Mountains: "We are now in just a small time of peace. No one knows what the future holds."

A small time of peace. This, in fact, was the general consensus I heard both in the Nuba Mountains and northern Bahr al-Ghazal as the long-anticipated signing of the comprehensive peace accord, the Naivasha Agreement,[1] between the Government of Sudan and the SPLM/SPLA drew near.

Implementation of the accords stretches out over more than half a decade, and, as many commentators have noted, the international community, which has driven the process, has a notoriously short attention span.

In that Khartoum eventually conceded most of its demands — *shari'a* law in the South, oil revenues, power sharing with rebel leaders — it's difficult, as Sudan expert John Ashworth recently noted, to see what the government gets from the deal. "Either they've had the most incredible conversion experience since St. Paul, or they're not serious about this."[2]

In the Nuba Mountains, the war has been effectively over for nearly three years now, cease-fire arrangements gradually solidifying into a kind of permanent peace. This, despite the fact that, even in the current peace negotiations, none of the basic political demands of the Nuba and other non-southern actors in the civil war would appear to have been definitively addressed.

The Nuba, currently, have been granted regional autonomy in a power-sharing arrangement between the government and the SPLM/A for a transitional period of six years — an arrangement that has "teeth" because both government and rebel military forces remain largely in place and because international monitors are vigorously involved. However, widespread skepticism persists about Khartoum's intentions in the Nuba Mountains, and what measures the government might take if the Nuba opt to secede with southern Sudan, should the South choose to take that course in the scheduled 2011 referendum, or demand some stronger form of regional autonomy than that envisioned in the current framework.

"The Nuba are surrounded," said Bronzino:

Their geographical position is in the North; their natural trading partners are there. The Nuba land is rich; there are natural resources. And the Nuba themselves are valuable to the north. The Nuba are strong workers, they're disciplined, there are all those colonies of Nuba in northern cities. I don't see how Khartoum can let the Nuba Mountains go.[3]

In the meantime, as a U.N. liaison and development officer with long experience in the Nuba Mountains told me, the most promising political developments in the whole country are happening in Nuba areas. More than 250,000 Nuba have returned to their villages in the "liber-

180

ated," or SPLA-held zones from the North or from government-held towns in the Nuba Mountains, reversing a fifty-year population drain in which enterprising Nuba left the *jebels* for the cities in search of education and jobs.

As I noted in my journal,

> In Arthur Howe's documentary "Kafi's Story,"[4] filmed just as the war in the Nuba Mountains began, his plucky Nuba hero, Kafi goes to Khartoum in search of work. At the film's conclusion the young man wonders aloud if future viewers of the film will ask, "Where is Kafi now?" Well, Kafi, scripted to lose his soul in the city and become a modern man has likely gone back to the mountains. History affords few cultures the chance to go home again.

More importantly, the official noted, belief in the vision of the "new Sudan," in political transformation in the north, not only as exemplified in SPLM chairman John Garang's platform, but in the Nuba's indigenous development of wartime democratic institutions, remains potent in the region. "If the SPLA can get its act together in the Nuba Mountains," he said, "possibilities exist that its example and prosperity can transform Arabized cultures and weaken the government's hold on power."[5]

In the South, I found a less complex political terrain. For one thing, the current peace accord specifies that the South will hold a referendum in six years to vote on whether to remain part of a united Sudan, or not.

"For most people," Stephen Myang Bol, a former SPLA commissioner for Twic County, told me,

> the war has simply gone on too long, the hatreds irreconcilable, the linguistic and cultural differences between North and South too deep for there to be a united Sudan. The only way we'll have a united Sudan is if it's forced on us by the big powers. My best guess is that we'll separate into north and south Sudan. In practical terms, we're already conducting our affairs without reference to the north. . . In fact, Sudan is disintegrating as we speak. Sudan is not a nation, that is to say a homogeneous culture; it is a country. The multiplicities of all our differences can't make us a nation.[6]

And then, there's Darfur.

The Darfur crisis, now a world-class humanitarian nightmare, seems, at least in political terms, both an epilogue to the long civil war between Khartoum and the SPLA, and a harbinger of future conflicts within Sudan even when the current peace agreement is signed.

While the Darfur rebellion didn't break out decisively until 2003, the conflict dates back to Khartoum's attempts to prevent the SPLA from gaining a foothold in the western province, as the insurgency had in the neighboring Nuba Mountains. As early as the 1980s, the government incited local Arab militias to attack southern Darfur's farming communities. Darfur's ethnic African tribes, in turn, formed self-defense groups, members of which coalesced into the two rebel movements, the Sudan Liberation Army (SLA), no relation to the SPLA, and the Justice and Equality Movement (JEM) that eventually rose against the government in February 2003.[7]

After a successful rebel assault on a military base in April of that year, Khartoum did what it has always done in such cases: it armed irregular militias, the aptly self-described *janjaweed* ("evil men on horseback") and, along with regular army troops, sent them in to crush the rebellion. This they proceeded to do by terrorizing civilian populations in the province, even those with no relation to the uprising, spreading death, rape, and destruction in every direction, with mass flight, disease, and famine following on the heels of attacks.[8] To date, more than 70,000 have died, with more than a million southern Darfuris at risk from the unfolding famine.[9]

The western media seems intent on viewing Darfur as an isolated atrocity; but, in fact, it's part of a much larger, and more complicated evil.

"When people talk about Sudan as a north-south conflict, they're wrong," Gassis told me in an interview before we left for Sudan:

It's not a struggle between Arab north and African south. The conflict is now and has always been fundamentally about ethnicities: An Arab Muslim elite pitting itself against African ethnic cultures, and this *throughout* the country, north and south, east and west. This is made clear when we consider that while the Nuba are religiously mixed, and the southerners are mainly Christian or followers of traditional belief, the people of Darfur are all *Muslims.* And yet this regime fights them. Why? For racial and ethnic reasons; because they are Africans, along with the Nuba, the Ingassena Hills people, the Beja, the Nubians and many others. This is the heart of the whole conflict; and this is meaning of Darfur.[10]

II

Tuesday, December 21
Kauda, Nuba Mountains
The plane pulled up to the end of the runway and shut down its engines — the exact spot from which we had scrambled on board that morning during the attack on the airstrip. It was odd, like having a chance to rewind an event, pulling luggage off the same plane, this time in reverse. We even piled into the same land cruiser, a vehicle that, by now, had earned a certain celebrity status. Not only did it have the "distinction" of being the first vehicle in the region, but the bishop's car had played a critical role in the SPLA's ability to mount a surprise attack on government troops during the May 2001 offensive, the last battle of the Nuba war. Call it an unofficial equipment loan.

I looked around.

A U.N. liaison officer friend had thought it only right to warn me about the *matatu*-style buses that now career over new dirt roads to Kauda — from former government-held towns like Kadugli, from as far away as Khartoum.

"You won't recognize the place," he had said.

From the tenor of his description, I was expecting black top and air traffic control towers; but, in fact, from what I could see, nothing had changed.

Nothing, that is, except a sign in English near a well just off the tarmac that announced in bold black letters:

"Congress man *[sic]* Frank Wolf Bore Well."

A plaque suited for the *new* Sudan, one could not help thinking: The Republican congressional leader from Virginia had been an early

War graffiti, Mayenabun, northern Bahr al-Ghazal, 2004

and vigorous champion of the use of American political muscle to impose a peace settlement on Sudan's warring parties — and this, long before it was fashionable.

Public signage, shifting honorifics: one of the first indications that new political realities are taking hold. I remember searching for the famous Gavrillo Princip footprints in downtown Sarajevo during the war. As a now-poignantly out-of-date guidebook describes it:

> The exact spot where Princip pulled the trigger [killing Austrian Archduke Franz Ferdinand, thereby igniting World War I] is marked by a slightly comical set of footprints, but as you stand there and look

184

out on what is really just an ordinary street corner, the weight of history, of being at the place where the straining muscles of Europe began to tear apart, hits you very hard.[11]

Well, it doesn't anymore — "hit you hard," that is. The reason I couldn't locate the memorial was that Sarajevo's embattled authorities, understandably cool in those days to Bosnian Serb gunmen, had had it torn up. The neighboring Princip museum, Princip Street, and Princip Bridge had undergone similar, if less drastic revisions.

There *were* changes visible from the airstrip, of course.

And not only the obvious ones: the still provisional architectural additions to the landscape, the new compounds of the nearly twenty international NGOs, their fleets of trucks and humming generators, which have come *en masse* to assist the Nuba with postwar reconstruction and development.

The real changes had to do with changes in perspective, in the angle of vision.

I was returning to *this* Nuba Mountains, the Nuba Mountains that had won for itself a degree of normalcy, as a stranger. In more than one later conversation, I caught myself lapsing into an apparently terminal state of reminiscence.

It didn't help that I had arrived to a necrology.

From my journal:

Nairobi.

The word came at lunch today with the bishop that Commander Mohamed Juma, the civil affairs administrator under Yusuf Kuwa, military hero of the Nuba war, died of liver cancer in Nairobi last Sunday [Dec. 12].

Father Sylvester Kasumba also passed away six months ago, in Uganda, of heart failure. He was in his forties.

I have also been warned discreetly that none of the parish priests I knew are still at their posts in the Nuba Mountains. Others have replaced them.

Father Tom is in Tanzania, a regional superior for the Maryknoll Missionaries now. The others, Father Solomon, Father Abraham, Father George, all of whom physically survived the war, were not, as it turned out, able to survive its interior consequences.

There is more than one kind of war casualty.

Wednesday, December 22
The Kauda market

There are few more efficient ways to survey Nuba life than to walk through one of the weekly agricultural markets that, outside of the periodic festivals, constitute the public life of Nuba villages.

Kauda has always boasted the largest of the area markets. Like the ones hosted by the other localities, Gidel's, for example, it is an all-day affair, held on the same day each week, always outdoors, and in a spot consecrated by long, though not necessarily immemorial custom.[12]

The best time for visiting markets in the Nuba Mountains, I'd always found, was in the morning, when farmers have just laid out their produce and temperatures are still cool. Due to time constraints, we were heading for Kauda, however, in the late afternoon, by which time a certain segment of the Nuba male population would have been quaffing *merissa*, the local sorghum beer, for much of the day, imparting to the market a certain woozy unpredictability.

That the agriculture was up and running, as officials had informed me, was apparent from the merest comparison of this kinetic bazaar spreading out over the hollows to the abandoned stalls and shriveled provisions of wartime.

I suppose it's only a matter of time until some well-meaning engineer suggests "permanent" structures for these movable feasts — stone, cement, and zinc roofing, no doubt — but the traditional market's labyrinth of dry-branch lattice-work, bleached reeds, and scrub brush partitions is, in my view, one of the masterpieces of indigenous Nuba architecture — all the more significant because of its impermanence, its "found" virtuosity.

A note from my journal:

There is a genius about living lightly on the land, in structures that make no claims against mortality, and that cannot offer to protect you from the earth.

The streaks of mica across the clay walls of my hut — original beyond imagination.

Though the harvest was past by the time we arrived, I still saw dried white beans, okra, potatoes, green onions, and the last of the tomatoes in the vegetable market, along with purple mounds of *karkaday,* dried hibiscus flowers used to make a traditional cold tea sweetened with sugar.

The newest postwar fashion in Nuba entertainment was much in evidence: a whole row of the market devoted to "tea houses," crowded booths in which fancy teas from Arab traders were served in small glasses along with leisurely conversation.

Modernity had arrived in the form of bicycles, now ubiquitous on roadways, t-shirts, Pepsi-Cola, cigarettes, and luxury soap.

The always numerous fakirs, purveyors of amulets, were less in evidence in this postwar market, but that's probably because there are fewer soldiers now. Guerilla fighters have a vested interest in miracles, in the claims, however improbable, attached to small leather pouches of herbs: amulets that I was once told offered protection, respectively, against landmines, hand grenades, and bullets.

I remember reading a report on state-owned television broadcasts in the North that, in order to increase enlistment in the army (always a problem for Khartoum, it seems), painted a similarly "angelic" picture of combat.

> Radio and television . . . talk of miraculous rains, of monkeys voluntarily embarking on mine-clearing operations, of martyrs who smell of musk and whose blood never clots, . . . armies transforming themselves into white horses, woods where trees whisper "Allah."[13]

*   *   *

It was already quite late, near sundown, when the wrestling match got underway at an open space at the west end of the market. Two teams of Tira and Otoro wrestlers were competing in what had to be among the first wrestling matches of a season that traditionally begins after the *dura* (sorghum) harvest in November.

The particulars of Nuba wrestling are strictly enforced, and Nadel's description of a Tira match he witnessed nearly seventy years ago could just as easily have described the contest I was watching:

> The [crowds] arrange themselves in two semicircles facing each other, representing the two hill communities whose young men are fighting that day. . . . The boys . . . who act as stewards and referees, carry sticks and twigs to drive the pressing crowd from the arena or threaten combatants who ignore their orders. They wear a dress as varied as it is colorful: aprons of goatskin, tassels of goat's hair, feathers, bells tied around the waist, and pieces of colored cloth tied to wherever pieces of cloth can be tied. . . . There is more much going on than just wrestling. When not engaged in a fight, the wrestlers are hopping about, singing and dancing. Others are blowing gourd trumpets and beating drums. Everything seems to happen at once. The . . . prefects pick out the fighters and send them into the ring, watching every step, shouting encouragement, ready to interrupt the fight if one or the other plays foul.[14]

The objective of Nuba wrestling is simple: when one has succeeded in tripping or throwing one's opponent on his back, the match is done. At its best, Nuba wrestling is more elegant test of cunning than display of brute strength. Bouts last seconds or several minutes at most, unless there is a draw, or the fighting becomes too intense, in which case, prefects intervene. Often, four or five bouts are going on at one time, with crowds surging in and out of the arena after each victory. In the context of a major festival, which this impromptu tournament was not, Nuba wrestling takes on an almost religious dimension, functioning, as Nadel asserts, as "occasions on which the whole tribe realizes and affirms its unity,"[15] the sacrament of Nuba culture.

This particular late December wrestling match ended up being, perhaps, a bit more revealing about the current challenges to Nuba unity than its sponsors may have intended.

Nuba wrestler, Kauda, 2004

188

Team of Nuba wrestlers, Kauda, 2004

As the crowd's excitement rose to a fever pitch of anticipation, managers, with a roar, suddenly whisked the two sets of wrestlers out of the arena. Their partisans followed, shouting bewildered praise. In a matter of minutes, the whole arena emptied without a single contest having been waged.

As it turned out, a very modern dilemma had called such an abrupt halt to the colorful proceedings. One of the young wrestlers, it seems, had demanded to know how just much money he would be paid for winning. Shocked local officials, citing a serious breach of tradition, promptly shut down the match.

Saturday, December 25 (Christmas Day)
Holy Cross Primary School, Kauda (renamed St. Vincent Ferrer)
After Christmas Mass, I slipped away from the crowds under the big ficus trees and trudged down the slope toward the memorial to the children of Kauda. It would be my only chance to visit the site of the attack, since we were leaving early the next morning.

As Mass was ending, the catechist Simon Kafi, the one whose fiancée had been killed in the bombing, came toward me through the crowd. I was delighted to see him, since I'd not had time in the short visit to look him up.

Simon is married now with two children.

"Where have you disappeared to?" he said as we greeted each other, referring, I supposed, to the three years I'd been away. "Please don't disappear like that again," he urged, quite seriously, with a hint of reproach. "At least write letters."

A little puzzled, I agreed nevertheless, and had turned to go, when he called after me:

"Don't you know that you are part of us?"

*   *   *

The schoolyard is unchanged, the old brick classrooms Father Sylvester had had built still standing, though the thatch looks in need of repair.

There was a fire at the school last year, arson, possibly. Some locals worried out loud that the act was politically or religiously motivated, an early warning shot in a behind-the-scenes campaign to "cut the Church down to size," to reduce its considerable influence in the new Nuba Mountains.

When I questioned Gassis, he dismissed the conspiracy theories, calling the fire merely "a personal vendetta, a wage dispute." But no one doubts that inter-communal divisions have gradually resurfaced during the years of the ceasefire, and, in some cases, would appear to be fueled from the outside.

A U.N. liaison officer in Nairobi told me that when the first large humanitarian convoys were sent into the Nuba Mountains, all the lorry drivers were found to be northern spies. In addition, he ticked off divi-

sions instigated by radical clerics newly attached to mosques in the Nuba Mountains, and recent disinformation campaigns waged against Abdel Aziz el-Hilu, the newly designated postwar governor of South Kordofan:

> The tensions are different than the tensions of the war years. Then, there was all this cohesion, the threat came from outside. Now the threat is inside as well. Things are much murkier here than they used to be.

Later that evening, I sat up with my oldest Nuba friend, the catechist Joseph Aloga, whom I'd met initially on my first night in the Nuba Mountains, at Christmas six years ago. We sat on folding chairs in the open courtyard of the Gidel parish compound, the setting of countless after dinner conversations, and talked through much of the night.

Joseph, originally from the village of Um Derdu, some two hours walk from Gidel, lives in Kauda now. His sixth child was recently born, and he is sporting a beard these days. He seems quieter, though, than I had remembered, sobered, though the gentle humor that originally drew me to him is never far.

Joseph's profile is a typical one: While he was the first Christian in his family, the result, ironically of time spent in Khartoum, his father is Muslim, some of his brothers are Christian, and there are traditionalists within his family.

In some ways, Joseph is the optimist among the "analysts" I consulted about Sudan's political future. Life is starting to go very well for the Nuba, he said.

> The people here have their doubts about the future, but they want the peace agreement to work, they really want a respite from the war, they want ordinary life to work for a while. They've had a taste with the ceasefire. The people are saying, We really have survived this, as if they don't quite believe it yet.

Joseph Aloga Jargi, Gidel, 2004

Even so, Joseph says,

> If there's trouble again, nobody here will ever surrender. Nobody will
> ever go back to the way things were before the war.

The shape of the future, the catechist declared, depends, in large part,
on what the North chooses to do. So far, he sees "a lack of good faith on
the part of the government," and, indeed, on the part of the country's
Arabs, as a whole.

> The government continues to say all the right things — reconcilia-
> tion, justice, a new start, and do all the wrong things — subvert, sow
> division, interfere with our freedoms.

Joseph shared his fears that if there were another war, "it will be much
worse than before."

> Now all the blacks [throughout the country] know what the situation
> is. Next time, there will be fighting everywhere.

On the other hand, said Joseph,

> Government Nuba are moving into the SPLM area, to be trained, to
> have freedom of speech, to be part of the "New Sudan." I have
> fought all my life for this, and, here in the Nuba Mountains, we al-
> ready live in the "New Sudan." The only issue is, finally, what its bor-
> ders will be.

And then he told me of recent Nuba attempts to negotiate with the
Baggara, the Arab cattlemen, the Nubas' traditional enemy, and, in the
war years, willing accomplices in Khartoum's decades of violence
against Nuba insurgents.

New hospital compound under construction, Gidel, Nuba Mountains, 2004

We can deal with the Baggara, we have a lot of experience. We are bringing them into the liberated areas. We are telling them that they, too, have been forgotten, that they must break with these patterns, and that we will help them. Some of them are listening. It will be a long process, but we will be very patient.[16]

"Loving your enemies," Bronzino had said, "it comes naturally to the Nuba. They have always lived on borders."

*   *   *

At the memorial:

Like the classrooms, it, too, looks a bit untended. Perhaps it's because I last saw the memorial cross when it was brand new, surrounded by school children and notables, the subject, briefly, of a flurry of international attention, that the effects of time and weather on the shrine seem unnerving.

The cement steps leading to the cross are wearing away now, scrubbed by Kauda's winds. Weeds have grown up around the base. The sides of the monument are beginning to settle into the sandy river soil, as the lettering on the cross

> "In Memory of our Martyred
> Children . . . Killed
> At this spot
> On Feb. 8, 2000 . . ."

fades more and more in the intense equatorial light. Nearby, the impact craters are erasing the memory of their deeds in drifting sand and grass. And black pigs scour for food in the shade of the tree where bombs once fell on a morning just like this.

Select Bibliography

African Rights. *Facing Genocide: The Nuba of Sudan*. London: African Rights, 1995.

———. *Justice in the Nuba Mountains of Sudan: Challenges and Prospects*. London: African Rights, 1997.

Aikman, David. "The World's Most Brutal, Least-Known War." *The Weekly Standard*, June 28, 1999.

Althaus, Dudley. "Watching Food Fly Away." *Houston Chronicle*, August 20, 1999.

Anderson, William, Roland Werner, and Andrew Wheeler. *Day of Devastation, Day of Contentment: The History of the Sudanese Church Across 2000 Years*. Nairobi: Paulines Publications Africa, 2001.

Baumann, Gerd. *National Integration and Local Integrity: The Miri of the Nuba Mountains in the Sudan*. Oxford: Clarendon Press, 1987.

Berry, Wendell. *The Art of the Commonplace: The Agrarian Essays of Wendell Berry*. Edited and introduced by Norman Wirzba. Washington, D.C.: Shoemaker & Hoard, 2002.

Broun, A. F. and R. E. Massey. *Flora of the Sudan*. London: Sudan Government Office, 1929.

Burr, Millard. *Quantifying Genocide in the Southern Sudan 1983-1993*. Washington, D.C.: American Council for Nationalities Service, 1993.

———. *Quantifying Genocide in Southern Sudan and the Nuba Mountains 1983-1998*. Washington, D.C.: American Council for Nationalities Service, 1998.

Burr, Millard, and Robert O. Collins. *Requiem for the Sudan: War, Drought & Disaster Relief on the Nile*. Boulder: Westview Press, 1995.

Deng, Francis Mading. *The Dinka of the Sudan.* New York: Holt, Rinehart, and Winston, 1972.

———. *War of Visions: Conflict of Identities in the Sudan.* Washington, D.C.: The Brookings Institution, 1995.

Faris, James C. *Nuba Personal Art.* Toronto: University of Toronto Press, 1972.

———. "Photographic Encounters: Leni Riefenstahl in Africa." Cape Town: Iziko Museum of Cape Town, 2002.

Finnegan, William. "The Invisible War." *The New Yorker,* January 25, 1999.

Fisher, Ian. "Can International Relief Do More Good Than Harm?" *The New York Times Magazine,* February 11, 2001.

Flint, Julie. "Democracy Under Fire." *Nafir,* January 1998.

———. "Government Offensive is aimed at Starving Out Rebels." *The Guardian,* June 4, 2001.

———. "Nuba Face Destruction." *The Guardian,* May 7, 2000.

Freedman, Ralph. *Life of a Poet: Rainer Maria Rilke.* Evanston: Northwestern University Press, 1996.

Gassis, Macram Max. "Pope John XXIII Lecture." *Catholic University of America Law Review* 4, Summer 2001.

Hasan, Yusuf Fadl, and Richard Gray, eds. *Religion and Conflict in Sudan: Papers from an International Conference at Yale University, May 1999.* Nairobi: Paulines Publications Africa, 2002.

Hass, Robert. *Twentieth Century Pleasures: Prose on Poetry.* New York: The Ecco Press, 1998.

Holt, P. M., and M. W. Daly. *A History of the Sudan: From the Coming of Islam to the Present Day.* Harlow, U. K.: Pearson Education Ltd., 2000.

Jok, Jok Madut. *War and Slavery in Sudan.* Philadelphia: University of Pennsylvania Press, 2001.

Judah, Tim. "The Stakes in Darfur." *The New York Times Review of Books,* January 13, 2005.

Kaplan, Robert D. *The Ends of the Earth: A Journey at the Dawn of the 21st Century.* New York: Random House, 1996.

Karrar, Ali Salih. *The Sufi Brotherhoods in the Sudan.* Evanston: Northwestern University Press, 1992.

Lacey, Marc. "Singers of Sudan Study War No More." *The New York Times,* July 12, 2004.

McKinley, James C. "Sudan's Calamity: Only the Starving Favor Peace." *The New York Times,* July 25, 1998.

MacMichael, H. A. *The Tribes of Northern and Central Kordofan.* Cambridge: Cambridge University Press, 1912.

Mackie, Ian. *Trek Into Nuba.* Edinburgh: The Pentland Press, 1994.

Malwal, Bona. "Sudanese Scholar Speaks Out." *Freedom Now News,* July 23, 2003.

Mahmoud, Mohamed. "Islam and Islamization in Sudan: The National Islamic Front." Washington, D.C.: United States Institute of Peace, 2004.

Mandani, Mahmood. "Whither Political Islam?" *Foreign Affairs,* January/February 2005.

Martin, James. "The Hidden Holocaust: An Interview with Sudanese Bishop Macram Max Gassis." *America,* January 15, 2000.

Miniter, Richard. "The False Promise of Slave Redemption." *The Atlantic Monthly,* July 1999.

Moorehead, Alan. *The Blue Nile.* London: The Folio Society, 2001.

————. *The White Nile.* London: The Folio Society, 2001.

Nadel, S. F. *The Nuba: An Anthropological Study of the Hill Tribes in Kordofan.* London: Oxford University Press, 1947.

Paz, Octavio. *The Other Voice: Essays on Modern Poetry.* New York: Harcourt Brace Jovanovich, 1990.

Picard, Max. *The World of Silence.* Chicago: Henry Regnery Co., 1952.

Rahhal, Suleiman Musa, ed. *The Right To Be Nuba: The Story of a Sudanese People's Struggle for Survival.* Lawrenceville, N.J.: The Red Sea Press, Inc., 2001.

Riefenstahl, Leni. *The Last of the Nuba.* New York: St. Martin's Press, 1995.

————. *The People of Kau.* New York: St. Martin's Press, 1997.

Rilke, Rainer Maria. *Ahead of All Parting: The Selected Poetry and Prose of Rainer Maria Rilke.* Edited and translated by Stephen Mitchell. New York: The Modern Library, 1995.

Rodger, George. *George Rodger: Photographic Voyager.* Petaluma: Barry Singer Gallery, 1999.

————. *Village of the Nubas.* Introduction by Peter Hamilton. Translated by Liz Heron. London: Phaidon Press, 1999.

Salih, Tayeb. *Season of Migration to the North.* Translated from the Arabic by Denys Johnson-Davies. London: Heinemann, 1981.

Saunders, William L. "Christmas in Sudan." *First Things,* May 1999.

————. "Grace Still More Abounds." *The Catholic World Report,* April 2000.

————. "The Slaughter of the Innocents." *The Catholic World Report,* May 1999.

Saunders, William, and Yuri Mantilla. "Human Dignity Denied: Slavery, Genocide and Crimes Against Humanity in Sudan." *Catholic University of America Law Review*, 51:3 (Spring 2002).

Scupoli, Lorenzo (Theophane the Recluse). *Unseen Warfare*. London: Faber and Faber, 1963.

Stevenson, R. C. *The Nuba People of Kordofan Province: An Ethnographic Survey*. Khartoum: University of Khartoum Graduate College Publications, 1984.

―――. "Some Aspects of Islam in the Nuba Mountains." *Sudan Notes and Records* 44 (1963).

Straus, Scot. "Sudan and Genocide." *Foreign Affairs*, January/February 2005.

Suliman, Mohammed. "Resource Access: A Major Cause of Armed Conflict in the Sudan — The Case of the Nuba Mountains." London: Institute for African Alternatives, 1998.

Taylor, John V. *The Primal Vision: Christian Presence Amid African Religion*. Philadelphia: Fortress Press, 1963.

Voll, John O. "Fundamentalism in the Sunni Arab World: Egypt and the Sudan." In *Fundamentalisms Observed,* edited by Martin E. Marty and R. Scott Appleby. Chicago: The University of Chicago Press, 1991.

―――. *Historical Dictionary of the Sudan*. Metuchen, N.J.: The Scarecrow Press, Inc., 1978.

Weekes, Richard V. *Muslim Peoples: A World Ethnographic Survey*. Westport, Conn.: Greenwood Press, 1981.

Winter, Roger. "The Nuba People: Confronting Cultural Liquidation." Washington, D.C.: U.S. Committee for Refugees, 2002.

Endnotes

Notes to the Introduction

1. Roger Winter, "The Nuba People: Confronting Cultural Liquidation" (Washington, D.C.: U.S. Committee for Refugees, 2002).

2. S. F. Nadel, *The Nuba: An Anthropological Study of the Hill Tribes in Kordofan* (Oxford: Oxford University Press, 1947), pp. 4-5.

3. African Rights, *Facing Genocide: The Nuba of Sudan* (London: African Rights, 1995), p. 11.

4. See Suleiman Musa Rahhal, ed., *The Right to Be Nuba: The Story of a Sudanese People's Struggle for Survival* (Asmara: The Red Sea Press, 2001), pp. 9-11, for a synopsis of the debate on linguistic linkages.

5. H. A. MacMichael. *The Tribes of North and Central Kordofan* (Cambridge: Cambridge University Press, 1912).

6. *Baggara* (Arabic for "cattle people") is the collective name for a number of nomadic Arab tribes, including the Misiriya and Hawazma.

7. African Rights, *Facing Genocide,* p. 17.

8. Mohammed Suliman, "Resource Access: A Major Cause of Armed Conflict in the Sudan. The Case of the Nuba Mountains" (London: Institute for African Alternatives, 1998).

9. R. S. O'Fahey, "They Are Slaves, but Yet Go Free: Some Reflections on Sudanese History," in *Religion and Conflict in Sudan* (Nairobi: Pauline Publications Africa, 2002).

10. Turabi, born in Kassala in eastern Sudan in 1932, comes from a family with a long history in academia and Sufism. Godfather of the Sudanese Muslim Brotherhood, a militant religious and political organization, he embarked on a political career in the mid-1960s, a career in which he has served as attorney general, justice minister, minister of foreign affairs, deputy prime minister, and Speaker of Parliament in a number of governments, while serving prison sentences during several others, notably under president Nimeiri. He fell out with fellow coup leader Omar el-Bashir in 1999, and is currently under house arrest.

11. Mohamed Mahmoud, "Islam and Islamization in Sudan: The National Islamic Front" (Washington, D.C.: United States Institute of Peace, 2004).

Notes to Chapter 1

1. Rainer Maria Rilke, *Ahead of All Parting: The Selected Poetry and Prose of Rainer Maria Rilke*, ed. and trans. Stephen Mitchell (New York: The Modern Library, 1995), pp. 551-52.

2. Talib Sayeh, *Season of Migration to the North*, trans. Denys Johnson-Davies (London: Heinemann, 1969), p. 167.

3. The distinction between Nuba and Nubian is discussed in the Introduction, p. 6.

4. Alan Moorehead, *The Blue Nile* (London: Hamish Hamilton, 1972), pp. 157-58.

5. Liner notes to Kronos Quartet, *Pieces of Africa* (Elektra, 1989). See also Hamza el-Din, *Escalay — The Water Wheel* (Nonesuch, 1971; reissued 2002).

6. Quoted in Jennifer E. Reed, "Sudan bishop says bombing is evidence of Christian persecution," Catholic News Service, February 15, 2000.

7. Rev. Hans Stuckelburger founded the Switzerland-based Christian Solidarity International in 1977 as a Christian human rights organization. CSI took a leading and sometimes controversial role in the practice of redeeming slaves in southern Sudan during the war.

8. In September 1983, Nimeiri, in concert with Islamist leaders, introduced *Shari'a*, or Islamic law as the law of the land, including use of the *hudud* — physical punishments such as flogging, amputation, stoning, and execution. This, coupled with the abrogation of the Addis Ababa Agreement, ending self-government in the South, sparked the second civil war (1983-2005).

9. African Rights, *Facing Genocide: The Nuba of Sudan* (London: African Rights, 1995), pp. 7-8.

10. Ian Fisher, "Can International Relief Do More Good Than Harm?" *The New York Times Magazine*, February 11, 2001.

11. *Jebel* is Arabic for "hill" or "mountain."

12. George Rodger, *Village of the Nubas* (London: Phaidon, 1955), pp. 31-32.

13. Roger Winter, "The Nuba People: Confronting Cultural Liquidation," (Washington, D.C.: United States Committee for Refugees, 2002), p. 9.

14. *Facing Genocide*, pp. 12-13.

15. Millard Burr, *Quantifying Genocide in Southern Sudan and the Nuba Mountains 1983-1998* (Washington, D.C.: American Council for Nationalities Service, 1998), p. xx.

16. Suleiman Musa Rahhal, ed., *The Right to Be Nuba: The Story of a Sudanese People's Struggle for Survival* (Lawrenceville, N.J.: The Red Sea Press, Inc., 2001), pp. 47-48.

17. Rahhal, *The Right to Be Nuba*, p. 2.

18. *Facing Genocide*, p. 1.

19. Speech delivered April 1, 2001, in Kauda, the Nuba Mountains. Copy in the author's possession.

20. S. F. Nadel, *The Nuba: An Anthropological Study of the Hill Tribes in Kordofan* (London: Oxford University Press, 1947), p. 1.

21. Nadel, *The Nuba*, p. 1.

22. Rodger, *Village of the Nubas*, p. 30.

23. Rodger, *Village of the Nubas*, p. 31.

24. Moorehead, *The Blue Nile*, p. 191.

25. Lorenzo Scupoli (Theophane the Recluse), *Unseen Warfare* (London: Faber and Faber, 1963), p. 196.

26. Robert Hass, *Twentieth Century Pleasures: Prose on Poetry* (New York: The Ecco Press, 1998), p. 230.

27. Rilke, *Ahead of All Parting*, pp. 551-52.

Notes to Chapter 2

1. Robert D. Kaplan, *The Ends of the Earth: A Journey at the Dawn of the 21st Century*, (New York: Random House, 1996), p. 5.

2. Ian Buruma, "Pioneer," *The New York Review of Books*, May 15, 2003.

3. P. M. Holt and M. W. Daly, *A History of the Sudan: From the Coming of Islam to the Present Day* (Harlow, U.K.: Pearson Education Ltd., 2000), p. 118.

4. S. F. Nadel, *The Nuba: An Anthropological Study of the Hill Tribes in Kordofan* (London: Oxford University Press, 1947), p. 5.

5. Interview in *The Magnum Story*, BBC2, October 1989.

6. George Rodger, *Village of the Nubas*, intr. Peter Hamilton, trans. Liz Heron (London: Phaidon Press, 1999), p. xx.

7. "George Rodger: Witness to Mystery," in *George Rodger: Photographic Voyager* (Petaluma, Calif.: Barry Singer Gallery, 1999), p. 10.

8. See, for example, Susan Sontag, "Fascinating Fascism," *The New York Review of Books*, February 16, 1975.

9. Rodger, *Village of the Nubas*, p. viii.

10. See, for example, James C. Faris, *Nuba Personal Art*, (Toronto: University of Toronto Press, 1972).

11. James C. Faris, "Photographic Encounters: Leni Riefenstahl in Africa" (Cape Town: Iziko Museum of Cape Town, 2002), p. 2. He is quoting Leni Riefenstahl, *The Sieve of Time: The Memoirs of Leni Riefenstahl* (London, Quartet Books, 1992). See also Faris's 1982 documentary, "The South-eastern Nuba" made for the BBC series *Worlds Apart*, which features a substantial critique of Riefenstahl's "people of Kau" photographs.

12. For more on this see Hamilton's introduction to Rodger, *Village of the Nubas*, viii.

13. Suleiman Musa Rahhal, ed., *The Right To Be Nuba: The Story of a Sudanese People's Struggle for Survival* (Lawrenceville, N.J.: The Red Sea Press, Inc., 2001), p. 42.

14. Leni Riefenstahl, *Last of the Nuba* (New York: St. Martin's Press, 1995) p. 20.

15. Leni Riefenstahl, *People of Kau* (New York: St. Martin's Press, 1997), p. 7.

16. Rodger, *Village of the Nubas*, p. iii.

17. Rainer Maria Rilke, *Ahead of All Parting: The Selected Poetry and Prose of Rainer Maria Rilke*, ed. and trans. Stephen Mitchell (New York: The Modern Library, 1995), p. 562.

18. Ralph Freedman, *Life of a Poet: Rainer Maria Rilke* (New York: Farrar, Straus, and Giroux, 1996), p. 532.

19. Rilke, *Ahead of All Parting*, pp. 192-93.

20. Robert Hass, *Twentieth Century Pleasures: Prose on Poetry* (New York: The Ecco Press, 1998), p. 261.

21. Octavio Paz, *The Other Voice: Essays on Modern Poetry* (New York: Harcourt, Brace, Jovanovich, 1990), pp. 145, 155.

Notes to Chapter 3

1. John V. Taylor. *The Primal Vision: Christian Presence Amid African Religion* (Philadelphia: Fortress Press, 1963), p. 10.

2. Ian Mackie, *Trek Into Nuba* (Edinburgh: The Pentland Press, 1994), pp. 129-30.

3. A. A. R. Saeed, "The Nuba," in *The Right To Be Nuba: The Story of a Sudanese People's Struggle for Survival*, ed. Suleiman Musa Rahhal (Lawrenceville, N.J.: The Red Sea Press, Inc., 2001), pp. 7-8.

4. Sudan, Africa's largest country, is slightly more than one quarter the size of the continental United States.

5. African Rights, *Facing Genocide: The Nuba of Sudan* (London: African Rights, 1995), p. 12.

6. African Rights, *Facing Genocide*, p. 13.

7. Saeed, "The Nuba," p. 11. See also H. A. MacMichael, *The Tribes of Northern and Central Kordofan* (Cambridge: Cambridge University Press, 1912), pp. 222-24.

8. Saeed, "The Nuba," pp. 7-8.

9. S. F. Nadel, *The Nuba: An Anthropological Study of the Hill Tribes in Kordofan* (London: Oxford University Press, 1947), pp. 9-14.

10. Richard V. Weekes, ed., *Muslim Peoples: A World Ethnographic Survey* (Westport, Conn.: Greenwood Press, 1984), p. 555.

11. It is widely believed that, overall, Nuba traditionalists (animists) predominate in some areas, while in others, especially around towns, Muslims are the majority, with Christians, of several denominations, a growing minority.

12. Videotaped interview with Mohamed Juma, December 23, 1998.

13. Gerd Baumann, *National Integration and Local Integrity: The Miri of the Nuba Mountains in the Sudan* (Oxford: Oxford University Press, 1987), p. 172; cited in African Rights, *Facing Genocide*, pp. 278-79.

14. Interview with Father Pasquale Boffelli, Nairobi, December 18, 2004.

15. R. C. Stevenson, "Some Aspects of Islam in the Nuba Mountains," *Sudan Notes and Records* 44 (1963), 1:19.

16. Nadel, *The Nuba*, p. 15.

17. Rahhal, *The Right to be Nuba*, pp. 72-84.

18. Interview with Ferdinand von Habsburg, Nairobi, December 1998.

19. African Rights, *Facing Genocide*, p. 122.

20. Report of the U.N. Special Rapporteur on Sudan to the 52nd Session of the U.N. General Assembly, December 1997. See also James C. McKinley, Jr., "Sudan's Calamity: Only the Starving Favor Peace," *The New York Times*, July 25, 1998.

21. African Rights, *Facing Genocide*, pp. 123-24.

22. African Rights, *Facing Genocide*, pp. 120-28.

23. Milliard Burr, *Quantifying Genocide in Southern Sudan and the Nuba Mountains 1983-1998* (Washington, D.C.: American Council for Nationalities Service, 1998), p. 32.

24. Baumann, *National Integration and Local Integrity*, p. 91.

25. Leni Riefenstahl, *The Last of the Nuba* (New York: St. Martin's Press, 1995), pp. 19-20.

26. African Rights, *Facing Genocide*, pp. 283-84.

27. Videotaped recording in the author's possession, December 24, 1998.

28. Apostles of Jesus was founded by Sisto Mazzoldi, Catholic Vicar Apostolic of Bahr al-Jebel Vicariate (Eastern Equatoria) until the missionary expulsion in 1964.

29. For a good popular account of Nubian Christianity, see Andrew Wheeler et al., *Day of Devastation, Day of Contentment: The History of the Sudanese Church Across 2000 Years*, (Nairobi: Paulines Publications, 2000), pp. 21-120.

30. Wheeler, *Day of Devastation*, pp. 175-77.

31. Wheeler, *Day of Devastation*, p. 469.

32. Interview with Father Butros Trille, Gidel, Nuba Mountains, December 24, 2004.

33. *Jellaba* (Arabic): Small-scale Arab merchants and traders operating throughout the Sudan.

34. African Rights, *Facing Genocide*, pp. 116-17.

35. African Rights, *Facing Genocide*, pp. 4-5.

36. African Rights, *Facing Genocide*, pp. 4, 206-95. For a full text of the fatwa of April 27, 1992, see pp. 289-91.

37. The "New Sudan" is the SPLM-SPLA's slogan for its stated commitment to a unified democratic, secular Sudan.

38. Interview with John Garang, Nairobi, December 1998. John Garang de Mabior (1945–2005) has been chairman of the SPLM/A since 1983. Born north of Bor in Upper Nile province, Garang pursued advanced studies in economics in the United States before undergoing military training at Fort Benning, Georgia, in the early 1970s. Garang returned to Sudan and held senior positions in the Sudanese military. When the Bor garrison mutinied in May 1983 amid renewed tensions between Khartoum and the South, President Nimeiri disatched Lt. Col. Garang to suppress the rebellion. The Bor native joined the mutiny instead, forming from its ranks the nucleus of the SPLA and its political wing, the SPLM. Despite early successes against government forces in the South and in coordinating political opposition to the NIF regime in the North, the SPLM/A was crippled by internal division over the movement's goals — national revolution or southern independence — and by a history of human rights abuses and charges of authoritarianism at the top. Khartoum was not slow to exploit these divisions, and internecine fighting between southern insurgents during the 1990s wreaked havoc on civilian popu-

lations in the South. By the turn of the century, a newly united SPLM/A, under Garang's leadership, entered into negotiations with Khartoum to end the war, leading eventually to the signing of a Comprehensive Peace Agreement in 2005. As part of the peace agreement, Garang was sworn in as first vice president of the Republic of Sudan under the terms of a new interim constitution in Khartoum on July 9, 2005. Three weeks later, Garang, on his way back from a diplomatic mission to Uganda, died in a helicopter crash in southern Sudan.

39. African Rights, *Facing Genocide*, p. 338.

40. African Rights, *Facing Genocide*, p. 311.

41. African Rights, *Facing Genocide*, pp. 338-339; see also *The Right to Be Nuba*, pp. 103-12.

42. David Aikman, "The World's Most Brutal, Least-Known War," *The Weekly Standard*, June 28, 1999.

43. Interview with Father Tom Tiscornia, December 25, 1998. Video copy in the author's possession.

Notes to Chapter 4

1. Quoted in Francis Deng, *War of Visions: Conflict of Identities in the Sudan* (Washington, D.C.: The Brookings Institution, 1995), p. 220.

2. The Turkana, Nilotic-speaking pastoralists, are the third largest tribe in Kenya, numbering between 250,000 and 340,000, and herd their flocks in a ever-expanding swath of territory covering most of northern Kenya.

3. Ruth Franklin, "God in the Details: Graham Greene's Religious Realism," *The New Yorker*, October 4, 2004.

4. Office of the United Nations Humanitarian Coordinator for Sudan, Press Release, June 24, 2003.

5. Dudley Althaus, "Watching Food Fly Away," *Houston Chronicle*, August 20, 1999.

6. Althaus, "Watching Food Fly Away."

7. Some relief agency estimates of the 1988 famine death toll range as a high as 500,000.

8. This has been documented by the U.S. Committee for Refugees.

9. Leni Riefenstahl, *The Last of the Nuba* (New York: St. Martin's Press, 1995), p. 75.

10. The Mahdist Revolution (1881-1885) was a mass revolt against Turko-Egyptian, and later British colonial rule inspired by "revivalist" leader Mohamed Ahmed ibn Abdullah who proclaimed himself God's divine leader (or *mahdi*).

11. P. M. Holt and M. W. Daly, *A History of the Sudan: From the Coming of Islam to the Present Day* (Harlow, U.K.: Pearson, 2000), 1:91.

12. J. Millard Burr and Robert O. Collins, *Requiem for the Sudan: War, Drought, and Disaster Relief on the Nile* (Oxford: Westview Press, 1995), p. 19. Much of this brief account of Sudan's food crisis is based on Burr and Collins's treatment.

13. Burr and Collins, *Requiem for the Sudan*, p. 19.

14. Burr and Collins, *Requiem for the Sudan*, p. 21.

15. Burr and Collins, *Requiem for the Sudan*, p. 114-15.

16. Ian Fisher, "Can International Relief Do More Good Than Harm?" *The New York Times Magazine,* February 11, 2001.

17. Wendell Berry, *The Art of the Commonplace: The Agrarian Essays of Wendell Berry,* (Washington, D.C.: Shoemaker & Hoard, 2002), p. 152.

18. Amnesty International, News Service Nr 32/02, February 22, 2002.

19. Burr and Collins, *Requiem for the Sudan,* pp. 312-13.

20. Fisher, "Can International Relief Do More Good Than Harm?"

Notes to Chapter 5

1. Gustav Mahler set this and four other elegies of the German poet Rückert (1788-1866) as the basis of his 1904 orchestral song cycle *Kindertotenlieder* (Songs on the Death of Children).

2. The notebook later became an icon of what came to be known as the "Kauda bombing," eventually forming the centerpiece of a display on religious and ethnic persecution in Sudan at the United States Holocaust Memorial Museum in Washington, D.C. in 2002.

3. The permanent diaconate was revived in the Roman Catholic Church after the Second Vatican Council. Usually married men, they remain permanently in the diaconate rather than proceeding on to priestly ordination. Their ordination allows them to perform certain liturgical and sacramental functions, such as preaching and administering baptism, but not to officiate at the Eucharist.

4. Yusuf Kuwa Mekki, "Things Were No Longer the Same," in *The Right To Be Nuba,* ed. Suleiman Musa Rahhal (Lawrenceville, N.J.: The Red Sea Press, Inc., 2001), p. 25.

5. African Rights, *Facing Genocide: The Nuba of Sudan* (London: African Rights, 1995), pp. 34-39.

6. David Tlapek and Gabriel Meyer, *The Hidden Gift: War & Faith in Sudan* (The Windhover Forum, 2000).

7. Gabriel Meyer, unpublished preliminary report, pp. 6-7.

8. Derek Hammond, unpublished report, February 26, 2000.

9. Rev. Renato Kizito Sesana, an Italian journalist and photographer.

10. Letter to Bishop Gassis from Rev. Thomas Tuscornia, February 16, 2000.

11. Stephen Amin, "Sudan: A Civil War Turned Against School Children," *Africanews,* February 2000.

12. "Albright 'outraged' by reports of Sudanese attacks on civilians," *Agence France Presse,* February 16, 2000.

13. Reuters, February 11, 2000.

14. Kakum led the devastating "Operation Long Jump" offensive in 1997. Rahhal, *The Right to Be Nuba,* p. 84.

15. Charles Ormondi, *Africa News,* February 18, 2000.

16. Jok Madut Jok, *War and Slavery in Sudan* (Philadelphia: University of Pennsylvania Press, 2001), p. 157.

17. "Sudanese Scholar Speaks Out," *Freedom Now News,* July 21, 2003.

18. Interview with John Deng Biong, acting commissioner, Twic county, December 28, 1998.

19. William Finnegan, "The Invisible War," *The New Yorker,* January 25, 1999.

20. Jok, *War and Slavery in Sudan,* p. 21.

21. For the debate on the practice of "redeeming" slaves, see Jok, *War and Slavery in Sudan,* pp. 153-79.

22. Interviews with "redeemed" children, Turalei, northern Bahr al-Ghazal, December 1998/April 1999.

23. Finnegan, "The Invisible War."

24. See Jok, *War and Slavery in Sudan,* pp. 100-101.

25. S. F. Nadel, *The Nuba: An Anthropological Study of the Hill Tribes in Kordofan* (London: Oxford University Press, 1947), p. 86.

26. The William Wilberforce Award is given annually by Prison Fellowship Ministries.

27. Telephone log, February 10, 2000. Notes on a conversation with R. Bronzino, relief coordinator, Nairobi.

28. Sudan Reflief & Rescue Press Release, February 11, 2000.

29. Newswire, Washington, D.C., February 14, 2000.

30. "US Condemns civilian bombings in Sudan," Reuters, March 8, 2000.

31. Tiscornia diary. Copy in author's possession.

32. Leni Riefenstahl, *The Last of the Nuba* (New York: St. Martin's Press, 1995), p. 174.

33. Max Picard, *The World of Silence* (Chicago: The Henry Regnery Company, 1952), p. 119.

34. Gabriel Meyer, "Yugoslavia's Agony of Soul," *National Catholic Register,* January 13, 1991.

35. Press Release, Diocese of El Obeid, Nairobi, April 8, 2000.

36. Bishop John Ricard of the Diocese of Tallahassee-Pensacola was the President of Catholic Relief Services at the time. He was originally scheduled to lead the delegation to the Nuba Mountains, hence the dedication.

37. Tiscornia letter to Gassis, February 16, 2000.

Notes to Chapter 6

1. Roger Winter, "The Nuba People: Confronting Cultural Liquidation" (Washington, D.C.: U.S. Committee for Refugees, 2002).

2. Yousif Kuwa Mekki, "Things Are No Longer the Same," in *The Right to be Nuba,* ed. Suleiman Musa Rahhal (Lawrenceville, N.J.: The Red Sea Press, Inc., 2001), pp. 31-32.

3. African Rights, *Facing Genocide: The Nuba of Sudan* (London: African Rights, 1995), p. 56.

4. Winter, "The Nuba People."

5. African Rights, *Facing Genocide,* p. 57.

6. Winter, "The Nuba People."

7. Julie Flint, draft of article on Yusuf Kuwa (unpublishied, November 29, 2001).

Endnotes

8. See Wheeler et al., *Day of Devastation,* pp. 646-51.

9. Wendell Berry, *The Art of the Commonplace: The Agrarian Essays of Wendell Berry* (Washington, D.C.: Shoemaker & Hoard, 2002).

10. Speech of Abdel Aziz Adam el-Hilu to the USCC Delegation to Sudan, April 1, 2001. Copy in author's possession.

11. African Rights, *Facing Genocide,* p. 66.

12. Anyanya (or Anya-Nya): This name for a poisonous insect in southern Sudan, and also a term for snake venom, was used to describe the military organization of the original southern Sudanese liberation movement, called (by 1963) the Sudan African National Union (SANU), which advocated southern secession. Originating in a mutiny of southern army officers in 1955, Anyanya waged a guerilla war against government forces in the south that was ended by the 1972 Addis Ababa Agreement. The so-called Anyanya II marked the first stages of the renewal of civil war in the south in 1983, and was eventually supplanted by the SPLA. Splits over reform or secessionist goals bedeviled both movements. See Francis Deng, *War of Visions: Conflict of Identities in the Sudan* (Washington, D.C.: The Brookings Institution, 1995), Chapter 5.

13. Diocese of El Obeid Press release, April 17, 2001

14. Abdel Aziz Adam el-Hilu speech.

15. Interview with Sister Gianfranca Silvestri, CMS, Lokichokio, Kenya, April 17, 2001.

16. Interview with Sister Anna Gastaldello, CMS, Lokichokio, Kenya, April 17, 2001.

17. SPLM/A press release, "GOS Dry Season Offensive Collapses," June 15, 2001.

18. Press Relase issued by the Office of the President Peace Adviser (Khartoum), January 19, 2002.

19. Text of the Nuba Mountains Cease Fire Agreement, Article II: 1-3.

20. Andreas Vogt, "The Sudan: Joint Monitoring Mission," 2004.

21. Vogt, "The Sudan."

22. Interview with Agostino el-Nur Ibrahim, Nairobi, December 29, 1998.

Notes to Chapter 7

1. Both this tale and the one on p. 9 are part of the folklore of the Tira Akhdar ("Green Tira"), a sub-group of the large Tira tribe in the southeastern jebels.

2. The agreement is named after the Kenyan resort of Naivasha, where it was signed on January 9, 2005.

3. Interview with Roberto Bronzino, Nairobi, December 19, 2004.

4. Arthur Howe and Amy Hardie, "Kafi's Story" (California Newsreel, 1989).

5. It should be noted that Abdel Aziz Adam el-Hilu has been appointed Governor of the newly constituted province of South Kordofan, thus promising solid leadership at least for this first phase of implementation.

6. Interview with Stephen Myang Bol, Turalei, northern Bahr al-Ghazal, December 27, 2004.

7. Motives for the Darfur insurgency are varied. One rebel group, the Sudan Liberation Army seems focused on classic complaints: government agricultural policies, lack of water, education and development. JEM, it would appear, has more Islamist aims. See Tim Judah, "The Stakes in Darfur," *The New York Review of Books*, January 13, 2005.

8. The displacement of civilians in order to fight rebels is a classic guerilla strategy: Once civilians are scattered, the "fish" (rebels) no longer have a "sea" (villages) in which to "swim" (operate).

9. By mid-October 2004, the World Health Organization estimates that 70,000 displaced persons had died of disease and malnutrition; the figure does not include violent deaths. An estimated 1.8 million, about a third of Darfur's population, had been uprooted by the war, with the majority displaced within Sudan, and approximately 200,000 in neighboring Chad.

10. Interview with Bishop Macram Max Gassis, Nairobi, December 17, 2004.

11. Martin Dunford, Jack Holland, et al., *Yugoslavia: The Real Guide*, (New York: Prentice-Hall, 1990).

12. For the view that Nuba markets, as such, may not date back much farther than the early decades of the twentieth century, see S. F. Nadel, *The Nuba: An Anthropological Study of the Hill Tribes in Kordofan* (London: Oxford University Press, 1947), p. 74.

13. Abdel Salam Sidahmed, "The Unholy War: Jihad and the Conflict in Sudan," in *Religion and Conflict in Sudan: Papers from an International Conference at Yale*, eds. Yusuf Fadl Hasan and Richard Gray (Nairobi: Paulines Publications Africa, 2002).

14. Nadel, *The Nuba*, p. 232.

15. Nadel, *The Nuba*, pp. 231-32.

16. Interview with Joseph Aloga, Gidel, Nuba Mountains, December 25, 2004.

Index